Communications in Computer and Information Science 1255

Commenced Publication in 2007
Founding and Former Series Editors:
Simone Diniz Junqueira Barbosa, Phoebe Chen, Alfredo Cuzzocrea,
Xiaoyong Du, Orhun Kara, Ting Liu, Krishna M. Sivalingam,
Dominik Ślęzak, Takashi Washio, Xiaokang Yang, and Junsong Yuan

More information about this series at http://www.springer.com/series/7899

Slimane Hammoudi · Christoph Quix ·
Jorge Bernardino (Eds.)

Data Management Technologies and Applications

8th International Conference, DATA 2019
Prague, Czech Republic, July 26–28, 2019
Revised Selected Papers

 Springer

Editors
Slimane Hammoudi
MODESTE/ESEO
Angers, France

Jorge Bernardino
Centre for Informatics and Systems
University of Coimbra
Coimbra, Portugal

Christoph Quix
Hochschule Niederrhein, University
of Applied Sciences
Krefeld, Nordrhein-Westfalen, Germany

Fraunhofer FIT
Sankt Augustin, Germany

ISSN 1865-0929   ISSN 1865-0937 (electronic)
Communications in Computer and Information Science
ISBN 978-3-030-54594-9   ISBN 978-3-030-54595-6 (eBook)
https://doi.org/10.1007/978-3-030-54595-6

This Springer imprint is published by the registered company Springer Nature Switzerland AG
The registered company address is: Gewerbestrasse 11, 6330 Cham, Switzerland

Preface

The present book includes extended and revised versions of a set of selected papers from the 8th International Conference on Data Science, Technology and Applications (DATA 2019), held in Prague, Czech Republic, from July 26–28, 2019.

DATA 2019 received 90 paper submissions from 36 countries, of which 9% were included in this book. The papers were selected by the event chairs and their selection was based on a number of criteria that included the classifications and comments provided by the Program Committee members, the session chairs' assessment, and also the program chairs' global view of all papers included in the technical program. The authors of selected papers were then invited to submit a revised and extended version of their papers having at least 30% innovative material.

The purpose of DATA 2019 was to bring together researchers, engineers, and practitioners interested on databases, big data, data mining, data management, data security, and other aspects of information systems and technology involving advanced applications of data.

We have selected eight papers for this book, which reflect also the main topics of the conference and the current trends in data science, technology, and applications. As data analytics plays a major role in current research and industrial applications, it is also the major topic in the selected papers. The first two papers address data analytics in text, i.e., sentiment analysis and text categorization. One of these papers also addresses the challenging issue of explainable AI as it aims at providing a human-readable explanation – why a text has been classified into a specific category. Four papers are in the area of data stream processing or sensor data processing. While three papers are application-oriented and address the challenges in data stream processing in Industry 4.0 and mobile communication traffic, the fourth paper proposes a scalable architecture for time series analysis systems. Deep learning is another topic addressed in the selected papers. One paper proposes an image processing method for farm detection in satellite images using convolutional neural networks. Finally, one paper discusses the fairness of performance comparisons for database systems. Some aspects that are raised in this paper should be considered in all evaluations in scientific papers in computer science in order to have fair evaluation results.

We would like to thank all the authors for their contributions and also the reviewers who helped ensure the quality of this publication.

July 2019

Slimane Hammoudi
Christoph Quix
Jorge Bernardino

Organization

Conference Chair

Jorge Bernardino   Polytechnic of Coimbra - ISEC, Portugal

Program Co-chairs

Slimane Hammoudi   ESEO, ERIS, France
Christoph Quix   Hochschule Niederrhein, University of Applied
                                   Sciences, Fraunhofer FIT, Germany

Program Committee

James Abello   Rutgers, The State University of New Jersey, USA
Maha Amami   University of Milan-Bicocca, Italy
Christos Anagnostopoulos   University of Glasgow, UK
Gustavo Arroyo-Figueroa   Instituto Nacional de Electricidad y Energías Limpias,
                                   Mexico
Karim Benouaret   Université Claude Bernard Lyon 1, France
Fadila Bentayeb   ERIC Lab, France
Jorge Bernardino   Polytechnic of Coimbra - ISEC, Portugal
Sukriti Bhattacharya   University College London, UK
Nikos Bikakis   University of Ioannina, Greece
Jan Bohacik   University of Zilina, Slovakia
Gloria Bordogna   CNR - National Research Council, Italy
Cinzia Cappiello   Politecnico di Milano, Italy
Sudarshan Chawathe   University of Maine, USA
Yixiang Chen   Software Engineering Institute, China
Chia-Chu Chiang   University of Arkansas at Little Rock, USA
Antonio Corral   University of Almeria, Spain
Gianni Costa   ICAR-CNR, Italy
Theodore Dalamagas   Athena Research and Innovation Center, Greece
Bruno Defude   IMT, France
Steven Demurjian   University of Connecticut, USA
Stefan Dessloch   Kaiserslautern University of Technology, Germany
Martin Drlik   Constantine the Philosopher University in Nitra,
                                   Slovakia
Fabien Duchateau   Université Claude Bernard Lyon 1, LIRIS, France
John Easton   University of Birmingham, UK
Todd Eavis   Concordia University, Canada
Zineb El Akkaoui   The National Institute of Posts and
                                   Telecommunications, Morocco

Neamat El Tazi	Cairo University, Egypt
Markus Endres	University of Augsburg, Germany
Francesco Folino	ICAR-CNR, Italy
Javier García	Vienna University of Economics and Business, Austria
Sandra Geisler	Fraunhofer FIT, Germany
Paola Giannini	University of Piemonte Orientale, Italy
Giorgos Giannopoulos	Athena Research and Innovation Center, Greece
John Gibson	IMT SudParis, France
Matteo Golfarelli	University of Bologna, Italy
Janis Grabis	Riga Technical University, Latvia
Aziz Guergachi	Ryerson University, ITM, Canada
Francesco Guerra	University of Modena and Reggio Emilia, Italy
Amarnath Gupta	University of California, San Diego, USA
Rihan Hai	RWTH Aachen University, Germany
Slimane Hammoudi	ESEO, ERIS, France
Andreas Henrich	University of Bamberg, Germany
Jose Herrera	Universidad del Cauca, Colombia
Ludmila Himmelspach	Heinrich-Heine-University Duesseldorf, Germany
Jang-Eui Hong	Chungbuk National University, South Korea
Tsan-Sheng Hsu	Institute of Information Science, Academia Sinica, Taiwan, China
Sergio Ilarri	University of Zaragoza, Spain
Ivan Ivanov	SUNY Empire State College, USA
Wang Jianmin	Tsinghua University, China
Christos Kalloniatis	University of the Aegean, Greece
Konstantinos Kalpakis	University of Maryland, USA
Dimitris Karagiannis	University of Vienna, Austria
Pawel Kasprowski	Silesian University of Technology, Poland
Mieczyslaw Kokar	Northeastern University, USA
Kostas Kolomvatsos	National and Kapodistrian University of Athens, Greece
Martin Krulis	Charles University, Czech Republic
Vladimir Kurbalija	University of Novi Sad, Serbia
Sarasi Lalithsena	IBM Almaden, USA
Jean-Charles Lamirel	LORIA, University of Strasbourg, France
Raimondas Lencevicius	Nuance Communications, USA
Christos Makris	University of Patras, Greece
Yannis Manolopoulos	Open University of Cyprus, Cyprus
Yuexin Mao	Deloitte Consulting, USA
Miguel Martínez-Prieto	University of Valladolid, Spain
Florent Masseglia	Inria, France
Marios Meimaris	Athena Research and Innovation Center, Greece
Amin Mesmoudi	Université de Poitiers, France
Yasser Mohammad	Assiut University, Egypt
Stefano Montanelli	Università degli Studi di Milano, Italy
Dariusz Mrozek	Silesian University of Technology, Poland

Erich Neuhold	University of Vienna, Austria
Antonino Nocera	University of Pavia, Italy
Riccardo Ortale	ICAR-CNR, Italy
Vincenzo Pallotta	HEIG-VD, Switzerland
Jisha Panackal	Sacred Heart College, India
George Papastefanatos	Athena Research and Innovation Center, Greece
Jeffrey Parsons	Memorial University of Newfoundland, Canada
Ilia Petrov	Reutlingen University, Germany
Nirvana Popescu	University Politehnica of Bucharest, Romania
Philippe Pucheral	University of Versailles Saint-Quentin en Yvelines, France
Paraskevi Raftopoulou	University of the Peloponnese, Greece
Werner Retschitzegger	Johannes Kepler University, Austria
Peter Revesz	University of Nebraska-Lincoln, USA
José Ríos Viqueira	Universidade de Santiago de Compostela, Spain
Colette Rolland	Université Paris 1 Panthéon-Sorbonne, France
Mercedes Ruiz	University of Cadiz, Spain
Gunter Saake	Institute of Technical and Business Information Systems, Germany
Dimitris Sacharidis	Technische Universität Wien, Austria
Iulian Sandu Popa	University of Versailles Saint-Quentin-en-Yvelines, Inria Saclay, France
Manuel Santos	Centro ALGORITMI, University of Minho, Portugal
Diego Seco	University of Concepción, Chile
Nematollaah Shiri	Concordia University, Canada
Marius Silaghi	Florida Institute of Technology, USA
Spiros Skiadopoulos	University of the Peloponnese, Greece
Dragan Stojanovic	University of Nis, Serbia
Sergey Stupnikov	IPI RAN, Russia
Zbigniew Suraj	University of Rzeszow, Poland
George Tambouratzis	Institute For Language and Speech Processing, Greece
Horia-Nicolai Teodorescu	Gheorghe Asachi Technical University of Iasi, Romania
Paolo Terenziani	Università del Piemonte Orientale, Italy
Catarci Tiziana	Università degli Studi di Roma La Sapienza, Italy
Raquel Trillo-Lado	University of Zaragoza, Spain
Christos Tryfonopoulos	University of the Peloponnese, Greece
Maurice van Keulen	University of Twente, The Netherlands
Michael Vassilakopoulos	University of Thessaly, Greece
Thanasis Vergoulis	Athena Research and Innovation Center, Greece
Karin Verspoor	The University of Melbourne, Australia
Marco Villani	University of Modena and Reggio Emilia, Italy
Gianluigi Viscusi	EPFL Lausanne, Switzerland
Zeev Volkovich	Ort Braude College, Israel
Leandro Wives	Universidade Federal do Rio Grande do Sul, Brazil
Robert Wrembel	Poznan University of Technology, Poland

Filip Zavoral   Charles University Prague, Czech Republic
José-Luis Zechinelli-Martini   Universidad de las Americas Puebla, Mexico
Jiakui Zhao   State Grid Big Data Center of China, China

Additional Reviewers

Victoria Döller   University of Vienna, Austria
Janis Kampars   Riga Technical University, Latvia
Jorge Silvestre   University of Valladolid, Spain

Invited Speakers

Manfred Reichert   Ulm University, Germany
Hans-Georg Fill   University of Fribourg, Switzerland

Contents

Explainable and Transferrable Text Categorization

Tobias Eljasik-Swoboda[1]([⊠]) [iD], Felix Engel[2] [iD], and Matthias Hemmje[2] [iD]

[1] Faculty of Mathematics and Computer Science, University of Hagen, Hagen, Germany
Tobias.Swoboda@fernuni-hagen.de
[2] FTK e.V. Forschungsinstitut für Telekommunikation und Kooperation, Dortmund, Germany
{fengel,mhemmje}@ftk.de

Abstract. Automated argument stance (pro/contra) detection is a challenging text categorization problem, especially if said arguments are to be detected for new topics. In previous research, we designed and evaluated an explainable machine learning based classifier. It was capable to achieve 96% F1 for argument stance recognition within the same topic and 60% F1 for previously unseen topics, which informed our hypothesis, that there are two sets of features in argument stance recognition: General features and topic specific features. An advantage of the described system is its quick transferability to new problems. Besides providing further details about the developed C3 TFIDF-SVM classifier, we investigate the classifiers effectiveness for different text categorization problems spanning two natural languages. Besides the quick transferability, the generation of human readable explanations about why specific results were achieved is a key feature of the described approach. We further investigate the generated explanation understandability and conduct a survey about how understandable the classifier's explanations are.

Keywords: Argument stance detection · Explainability · Machine learning · Trainer-athlete pattern · Ontology creation · Understandability support vector machines · Text analytics · Architectural concepts

1 Introduction

The goal of the RecomRatio project is to implement an information system for supporting medical professionals. This support comes in the form of recommendations for treatment options in combination with rational arguments why specific treatments are suggested. In the envisioned system, the recommendation is going to be based on an argument ontology containing entire pro and contra arguments for given topics in medicine. These arguments are sourced from concrete clinical studies and other publicly available data sets like PubMed [1]. The ability to explain why certain recommendations were generated is important due to two reasons: Firstly, patients and medical practitioners have more confidence in a recommendation if they can inspect the reasons for this argument. Secondly, the European Union's (EU) General Data Protection Regulation

© Springer Nature Switzerland AG 2020
S. Hammoudi et al. (Eds.): DATA 2019, CCIS 1255, pp. 1–22, 2020.
https://doi.org/10.1007/978-3-030-54595-6_1

(GDPR) contains a right to explanation [2]. This piece of legislature grants every EU citizen the right to demand explanations for the results of machine learning (ML) and artificial intelligence (AI) systems if they are impacted. Up until recently, this has not been an aspect of ML and AI research [3]. At the time of writing this article, PubMed contained over 30,000,000 medical abstracts and links to the actual papers and studies [1]. Manually assessing this much data and modeling its contents into ontologies is not feasible. To overcome this bottleneck Argument Mining (AM) is employed.

Research in Argument Mining aims to automate the detection of arguments in large amounts of text. It combines a broad set of computer science sub disciplines such as Natural Language Processing (NLP), Artificial Intelligence (AI) and Computational Linguistics [4]. A specific challenge within Argument Mining is the detection of an argument's stance. This means whether it is pro or contra to a specific topic. At the Semeval16 conference, multiple stance detection approaches have been evaluated [5]. Detecting the stance of arguments about previously unseen topics is more challenging than detecting them in known topics.

This paper is the extended version of a conference paper in which we described an explainable, machine learning based classifier, called C3 TFIDF-SVM, which was evaluated using two argument stance detection datasets [6]. The C3 TFIDF-SVM classifier is intended as part of the argument mining environment used to create the RecomRatio argument ontology. The developed classifier was capable to achieve .96 F1 within the same topic and $>.6$ F1 for different topics. This informed our following hypothesis:

There are two sets of terms that serve as argument stance features:

1. *The set of general argument stance feature G.*
2. *The set of topic specific argument stance features F(t).*
   If one has G and F(t) for topic t along with a machine learned model for the combination of these features, high effectiveness, explainable classification can be achieved. If one works with another topic, F(t) becomes noise decreasing overall effectiveness.

This article provides further details about the C3 TFIDF-SVM and analyzes our hypothesis. C3 TFIDF-SVM has the additional advantage of being quickly transferable to other TC problems. Therefore we tested it on four different TC problems across two natural languages and evaluated its performance. Additionally, we conducted a survey about how understandable the generated explanations are.

The remainder of this article is structured as follows: Section two describes the state of the art and technology relevant for the creation of C3 TFIDF-SVM. Section 3 provides details about the underlying model used for C3 TFIDF-SVM. Section 4 details its implementation. Section 5 contains an effectiveness evaluation across multiple problems while Sect. 6 contains our survey results about the generated explanations' understandability. Section 7 finishes with conclusions about our research.

2   State of the Art

2.1   Argument Mining

As previously explained, Argument Mining or Argumentation Mining aims to automate the detection of arguments in large amounts of text. Besides the detection of arguments related to specific topics, detection of the argument stance is a specific challenge. In 2016, the association for computational linguistics created the *detecting stance in tweets* challenge. The results were published in the proceedings of SemEval-2016 [5]. For this challenge, 4,870 English tweets for stance towards six commonly known topics in the United States were annotated with *favor* and *against*. These topics were *Atheism, Climate Change is a Real Concern, Feminist Movement, Hillary Clinton* and *Legalization of Abortion*. Here, 70% of the annotated data was provided for training while the remaining 30% were reserved for testing. 16 Teams submitted classifiers for this task where the highest F1 result was 67.82%. It was achieved by employing two recurrent neural network classifiers in concert. This however was below the baseline classifier created by the challenge's organizers which achieved 68.98% F1 by using a linear kernel Support Vector Machine (SVM) (see Sect. 2.2) classifier per topic that used word n-grams (1-, 2-, and 3-gram) and character n-grams (2-, 3-, 4-, and 5-grams) as features [7]. This was subsequently tuned using 5-fold cross-validation on the available training data. To the best of our knowledge, no further feature selection took place, providing the SVM with a high dimensional problem. It is noteworthy, that this comparatively simple baseline model outperformed many more advanced classifiers using deep learning or word embeddings (see Sect. 2.2).

For the second task of the challenge, the new topic *Donald Trump* was introduced. Here, no labeled training data was provided and the classifiers trained on the previous topics were tasked with classifying tweets towards this new topic. The best participant achieved 56.28% F1. The baseline system was used in two ways: Firstly, a majority vote of all individual SVMs regarding the stance of the new topic was performed. Secondly, one SVM was trained with training samples across all different topics. The Majority Baseline classifier achieved 29.72% overall F1. Interestingly, it hat an F1 of 59.44% for identifying the *against* sentiment while that to identify the *favor* sentiment is 0.

In their work Stab et al. created the UKP Sentential Argument Mining Corpus (UKP) including over 25,000 instances over eight topics by querying Google regarding these topics and having crowd workers annotate Google's preview texts [8]. The UKP corpus covers the topics *abortion, cloning, death penalty, gun control, marijuana legalization, minimum wage, nuclear energy* and *school uniforms*. Using a LSTM based classifier, Stab et al. were able to achieve F1 of 66.62% within the same topic. Some interesting experiments with the training set were performed. The classifier was evaluated with a single topic. It was trained on a mix of arguments containing different percentages of target topic samples. 20% of target topic data already have strong positive effects on recall (see Sect. 2.3).

Another task in this context is same side stance classification. Here, two arguments are used as input and a classifier has to determine if both have the same or different stances. Within the same topic, F1 values of 77% are state of the art. In different topics, F1 values of 73% were achieved [9].

There are multiple other works in the field of argument mining which cannot feasibly be covered in a single article. The illustrated works however show the following findings: Firstly, argument stance recognition is hard. State of the art systems struggle to achieve >70% F1. Secondly, argument stance recognition is even more difficult when a classifier is created using one set of topics but is subsequently applied to another topic.

Thirdly, even though SVMs have been around for a long time and linear kernels are the simplest implementation of SVM; they are surprisingly highly effective compared to more sophisticated classifiers.

2.2 Text Categorization Approaches

The formal definition of Text Categorization (TC) is that a classifier $\Phi: (D, C) \to \{0, 1\}$ approximates a target function $\Phi': (D, C) \to \{0, 1\}$ as closely as possible [10]. Here the set D contains relevant documents and C the categories they are assigned to. For the argument stance recognition problem, D consists out of individual arguments and C of *pro* and *contra*. Of course there are a multitude of different NLP problems that can be modelled as TC problem. Among these problems are *intent detection* for chatbots or *hate speech detection* for social media applications.

The set of available assignments $\Omega = \{\Phi', D, C\}$ is also referred to as *initial corpus*. For research purposes Ω is oftentimes split into training sets *TS* and evaluation sets *ES* so that $TS \cap ES = \emptyset$. While *TS* is used to create Φ, *ES* is used to evaluate its effectiveness using different metrics described in Sect. 2.3. If no predetermined split between *TS* and *ES* is available, one can also use the *n-fold cross-validation* process. Here, Ω is split in n subsets of about equal size. In the next step, n different classifiers are created, each of which are created with a different combination of $(n - 1)$ subsets so that the remaining subset can be used as *ES*. One can of course perform n-fold cross-validation on a predetermined training set and then apply the best performing model to the actual evaluation set of a specific task. For practical applications, the evaluation set is the real life productive application of the classifier in an application.

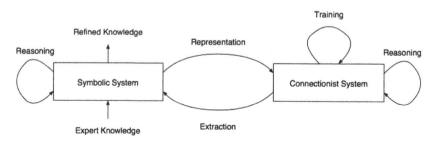

Fig. 1. Illustration of nerual-symbolic integration [11].

There are two fundamental approaches of how to implement TC: One can either used fixed rules or apply machine learning to the problem [10]. The combination of both is referred to as neuro-symbolic integration (see Fig. 1) [11]. For rule based TC, experts need to create rules which a machine can use to determine the correct category. To do so, texts are checked for the occurrence of certain terms which can be simple words or more complex regular expressions describing entire sentences [10, 12].

Most machine learning based classification algorithms are defined for numeric input [10]. Therefore machine learning based text categorization occurs in three phases each of which can be implemented using different algorithms or algorithms spanning multiple of these phases:

1. Phase: Feature extraction: Text is transformed into feature vectors comprehensible for machine learning algorithms.
2. Phase: Feature selection. Reduction of the feature vector size to speed up and enhance the effectiveness of machine learning
3. Phase: Machine learning based text categorization.

For practical applications, one has to distinguish between the training of classifiers, or models, that then work on productive data during inference. Popular approaches for the implementation of machine learning are simulated neural networks [13, 14]. Deep learning was originally defined as using cascades of multiple machine learning approaches but has since also become synonymous with artificial neural networks that use more than three layers or neurons between in- and output. These approaches are so popular that they have become synonymous with machine learning and artificial intelligence albeit multiple other highly effective approaches exist [15]. One such alternative are Support Vector Machines (SVMs) [16]. These operate by projecting input data points into high-dimensional spaces which are bisected by a hyperplane. If the points are above the hyperplane they belong to the category, if not they are not, they don't belong to the category. Training the hyperplanes from samples is performed by maximizing the margin between the hyperplanes and the closest vectors. As only the closest vectors are taken into consideration, these are also referred to as support vectors. In order to cope with non-linearly separable datasets, SVMs can work with slack variables that essentially allow for certain vectors to be a little bit on the wrong side of the hyperplane. Additionally, they can work with alternative kernels. In the context of SVMs, kernels are alternative implementations of the dot-product which is required to compute the relative location of a data point related to the hyperplane. Changing its computation allow for curved hyperplanes that essentially project data into higher dimensional spaces so that it can be bisected with a hyperplane there. As Sect. 2.1 has shown, even linear kernel SVMs (where the dot product simply is the dot product) were able to outperform sophisticated neural networks in certain argument mining tasks. A common library for the implementation of Support Vector Machines is LibSVM [17].

With regards to TC, SVMs are phase 3 algorithms. Their performance largely depends on how data points are represented to them. A straight forward approach is to count how often certain terms occur in each text and use these values as feature vector. This is referred to as the Bag of Words (BoW) approach. One can fine-tune it by providing a controlled vocabulary of relevant terms to spot. One however needs to normalize these vectors so that the generated vectors are of equal length. More complex approaches are to use word n-grams (*n* words occurring after each other) and character n-grams (*n* single characters occurring after each other) as features. This can quickly lead to highly dimensional text representations which in turn require large amounts of computational resources for training and inference. An alternative are Word Embeddings. This class of unsupervised learning algorithms uses unlabeled text to represent terms with coordinates which encode their relationship to each other based on their offset. For instance, the offset between terms of different gender like *man, woman, boy, girl, king,* and *queen* are all similar. Notable implementations are Word2Vec's CBOW, skip-gram, and GloVe [18, 19]. During the training of word embeddings, individual texts can also be represented by a vector. This however is not possible during inference. The problem of grouping a sequence of word vectors into a single vector representative of the sequence is called Compositional Distributional Semantics (CDS) [20]. Multiple approaches such as the Basic Additive Model or the Word Mover's Distance (WMD) have been proposed [21]. These have been used to implement entirely unsupervised classifiers that work by assessing the distance between categories and texts [22, 23].

Another notable approach to feature extraction is the use of neural network based encoders/decoders. Their aim is to transform terms into numeric vectors and vice versa. Different from word embeddings, these encoders take the ordering and accompanying words into account. This allows it to determine what words like *it* in a sentence refer to [24]. BERT is available as pre-trained model that was created in an unsupervised fashion. The model can subsequently be used in any NLP application. BERT models are huge. The BERT_large model has 345 million individual parameters making up the network. The BERT_base model still has 110 million parameters. Both are highly obscure meaning that their results are next to impossible to explain.

As initially stated, the explainability of generated results is a comparatively novel requirement that has not been in the focus of NLP research until recently. In principle, researchers and programmers that are intimately familiar with their algorithms and have access to their internal state at run time, for instance by accessing log files, can provide explanations why certain results were created. This is however insufficient for practical applications because the internal state usually is not logged and the creators of algorithms are not the organizations operating them and having to explain why certain results were generated. Operating organizations actually require a system that can automatically create explanations for generated results. Lexicon based classifiers, such as *ReLexNet*, are a class of such easily explainable classifiers [3]. These comparatively simple constructs function by creating an association matrix between individual terms and categories. The likelihood of a document to belong to a specific category is based on how many terms of high association with this category occur within the document. These terms can be influenced by modifier and negator terms. Negators multiply the term's association with -1. Strength modifiers like *little* can reduce or boost an association value, for example by 0.3. Explanations can be generated by stating which terms were found within the documents. A drawback of lexicon based classifiers are, that they require manually created lexica of at least modifier terms. Additionally, they can have issues with linear separability, as two words individually might indicate a certain category but in combination would contra indicate it. This is difficult to model using only a lexicon.

As described in this section, there are many options and considerations when implementing a TC application like argument stance recognition. The Cloud Classifier Committee (C3) was developed to make TC easily available to any application. To make TC as simple as accessing an external database, C3 was implemented as modern and flexible microservice-oriented architecture [6, 12, 25]. C3 provides TC capability through a simple REST/JSON interface. Notably, this interface caters to generate explanations for created categorizations. To do so, the trainer/athlete pattern for microservice oriented machine learning is used (see Fig. 2).

With the trainer/athlete pattern, a trainer service computes a model that can be used by any athlete service. As applied inference can be time critical for certain applications, the athlete services are stateless after having been provided with a model. This way one

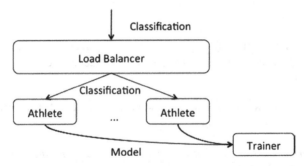

Fig. 2. The trainer/athlete pattern for microservice-oriented machine learning [6].

can easily scale-out the application as required. As TC uses common API endpoints, one can combine different C3 microservices into committees of automated classifiers.

2.3 Feature Assessment and Evaluation Metrics

Feature rating, assessment, selection and extraction as used in this publication build on concepts from the Information Retrieval (IR) community. To evaluate the ability of an IR system in a specific task the two basic metrics *precision* and *recall* are used. Precision is defined as the proportion between the intersection of relevant and retrieved documents to retrieved documents. One could say it is the percentage of correctly retrieved documents. In contrast to precision, recall is defined as the proportion of the intersection between relevant documents and retrieved documents to relevant documents. In other words the percentage of how many documents were retrieved to how many documents should have been retrieved. Both measures are excellent to gauge how correct a TC system operates for a specific category. The F1 score is the harmonic mean between precision and recall. One can for instance have perfect recall but poor precision by assigning every document to one category. A low F1 value shows such shortcomings. TC is oftentimes performed for more than one category. There are two different methods for averaging result scores: In Microaveraging, individual true positives, false negatives and false positives of each category are summed up and global precision, recall and F1 scores are calculated. In Macroaveraging, the results of all individual categories are averaged [10].

The *Term Frequency Inverse Document Frequency* is a statistic value used to indicate how representative a term is for a specific document (see Eq. 1).

$$tfidf\left(t_k, d_j\right) = \#\left(t_k, d_j\right) * \log\left(\frac{|TS|}{\#TS(t_k)}\right) \tag{1}$$

TFIDF is computed by counting how often a specific terms t_k occurs within document d_j ($\#(t_k, d_j)$) and multiplying this value with the logarithm of the quotient between the training set size ($|TS|$) and the amount of documents in the training set that contains term t_k. This formula models two intuitions: Firstly, if a term occurs oftentimes within the same document, it is very representative for the document. Secondly, if a term occurs in many documents, it cannot be representative for any document. If a term occurs in all documents, it has a TFIDF value of 0.

3 Model

The goal for our model is two-fold. Firstly, we aim to create an explainable classifier for argument stance recognition. Secondly, we want to identify relevant features for the identification of topic specific arguments.

If a classifier has sets G and $F(t)$ of topic specific and general features (see Sect. 1), it could generate explanations for categorization decisions based on found features within the text. Explanations can be stored in sentences like:

> *"The argument is considered contra, because it contains multiple occurrences of the terms tragedy, leaks, soldiers and blood. These terms have been detected as contra indicators in the given data set containing 27,538 arguments about the topic policy"* [6].

Having multiple topic specific data sets enables the creation of an argument stance feature ontology by identifying sets of relevant features and comparing these features with each other. As shown in Fig. 3, a concept can be an argument stance feature which can either be topic specific or general. In any case, it was extracted from a specific corpus of documents which in turn is specific to a topic.

To achieve our goals, we require a model that can automatically detect relevant features for argument stance recognition. To do so, we implemented the C3 trainer/athlete pattern. When creating a model, the trainer is provided with an initial corpus of labeled arguments. Based on this corpus, the TFIDF value for every term t_k is computed. To do so, the word occurrences in all documents are counted. No filters like stop word lists or predefined n-gram lists are applied as the goal overreaching concept of C3 is to make TC as accessible as possible by requiring no additional resources but the training set. Stop word lists are almost superfluous as stop words have low TFIDF values as they occur in almost all documents.

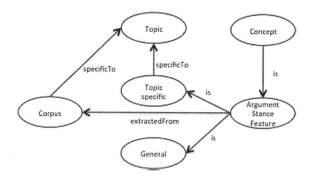

Fig. 3. Structure of a topic specific argument stance feature ontology [6].

After computing the TFIDF values, relevant feature terms must be identified. This is done by identifying the h highest TFIDF values for documents belonging to each category. We chose 20 as default value for this configurable parameter. This means that h relevant terms per category are added to an automatically created controlled vocabulary.

In the next step, this list of relevant features is augmented by the single highest TFIDF term of every available document if it is not already within this list. This approach creates a list of word 1-grams that serve as features for the TC task the list was created for.

We chose to use LibSVM with a linear kernel as machine learning based classification approach because of multiple reasons: Firstly, linear kernel SVMs have been reported to perform better than many more sophisticated approaches in argument mining (see Sect. 2.1). Secondly, SVMs are relatively easy to explain: If a feature vector is above the hyperplane, the document belongs to the category. Thirdly, SVMs require comparatively little computational resources and their stored models are highly portable as the hyperplane can easily be stored and transferred to other machines.

LibSVM requires its feature vectors to be normalized per dimension. This means, that in all feature vectors of a corpus, the scalars representing an individual term (i.e. *tragedy*) must have a combined length of 1. LibSVM also requires sparse vectors consisting out of arrays containing topics of the dimension and value for this dimension. To create this representation, the dimension is specified by the term's id within the controlled vocabulary. The value is the normalized TFIDF value. Formula 2 provides the necessary dimensionally normalized value.

$$ntfidf\left(t_k, d_j\right) = \frac{\#\left(t_k, d_j\right) * \log\left(\frac{|TS|}{\#TS(t_k)}\right)}{\sqrt{\sum_{i=1}^{|D|}\left(tfidf\left(t_k, d_i\right)\right)^2}} \tag{2}$$

During training, this is easily computed, as the original TFIDF matrix for selecting relevant features is still available. In order to use this scheme during inference in an athlete service, one must take into account that every document from which features are extracted is actually the first one after |TS|. This changes part of the original TFIDF equation from $\frac{|TS|}{\#TS(t_k)}$ to $\frac{|TS|+1}{\#TS(t_k)+1}$. As the trainer service does not contain the original TFIDF matrix, the transferred model must contain $\sqrt{\sum_{i=1}^{|D|}\left(\#(t_k, d_i) * \log\left(\frac{|TS|+1}{\#TS(t_k)+1}\right)\right)^2}$ for each term t_k. This way, inference in an athlete service can use formula 3 because the denominator, |TS| and $\#TS(t_k)$ are stored in the model:

$$itfidf\left(t_k, d_j\right) = \frac{\#\left(t_k, d_j\right) * \log\left(\frac{|TS|+1}{\#TS(t_k)+1}\right)}{\sqrt{\sum_{i=1}^{|D|}\left(\#(t_k, d_i) * \log\left(\frac{|TS|+1}{\#TS(t_k)+1}\right)\right)^2}} \tag{3}$$

For training, n-fold cross-validation on the initial corpus is performed. This creates n models each of which is evaluated with a different evaluation set. Afterwards, the trainer selects the model of highest effectiveness. Which effectiveness measure is used can be selected. The default value is microaverage F1 (see Sect. 2.3). The best performing TFIDF model as well as the controlled vocabulary and the afore-mentioned relevant values of formula 3. This creates a compact model that is freely transferrable from trainer to athlete services without transferring the training set. As it contains a list of relevant terms to use as features, these terms can be used to generate explanations as well as to create the argument feature ontology shown in Fig. 3.

4   Implementation

Based on the utilized technologies, we refer to our classifier as C3 TFIDF-SVM. The trainer/athlete pattern and all required interfaces are implemented as REST/JSON endpoints. These endpoints provide Create, Read, Update and Delete (CRUD) operations which can be triggered using the http POST, GET, PUT and DELETE verbs. These endpoints are application independent and cater for documents, categories, category relationships (hierarchical categories are possible), manual assignments (the target function), categorizations (the athlete's results) created models and their effectiveness evaluations for the trainer and actively used model for the athlete. Additionally, a metadata endpoint provides information about the service. Besides these endpoints, C3 services also include a web GUI which controls the service using the endpoints and is hosted on it. The categorization objects link documents with their categories and additionally contains a human readable explanation. An advantage of the JSON objects are the relatively simple human readability which allows us to inspect which terms were selected to be used as features.

We implemented the services in Java using the Dropwizard framework [26]. This approach allows us to package the classifier as fat jar file which can be run on any device that support Java and has a network interface. There is only one additional YML file required which contains parameters such as the network port the service is listening on. In terms of machine learning libraries, only LibSVM was used. We implemented the described feature extraction and selection scheme directly. In addition to this jar packaging, we additionally packaged the services as docker containers in order to minimize deployment time on arbitrary environments [27].

Another part of C3 is an API library that can be used in java in order to access the C3 endpoints. This is however completely optional, as all experiments can also be performed via the web-GUI. Using the library is however much more convenient for thousands of arguments to be uploaded.

As shown in Fig. 4, the TFIDF-SVM service was executed on a Linux server provided by the university that was accessed by a personal computer similar to how a piece of software accesses a central database. A Microsoft Azure Container Registry was used to store the container which necessitated the installation of the Microsoft *az* command line utility on the server. This setup underlines the flexibility of C3 as Apple, Microsoft and Linux systems were easily combined.

The TFIDF-SVM trainer automatically performs n-fold cross-validation and provides effectiveness results obtained during the training of a model. If the created model is to be evaluated with previously unseen arguments, an athlete service is provided with the created model. Instead of implementing an additional evaluation component, the C3 committee service is used. This service forms a committee of multiple athletes. As combination function, it measures the effectiveness of utilized athletes with all known documents. The results are subsequently weighted according to their effectiveness. If only a single athlete is provided, the C3 committee only measures the effectiveness of this single athlete which is then stored for inspection.

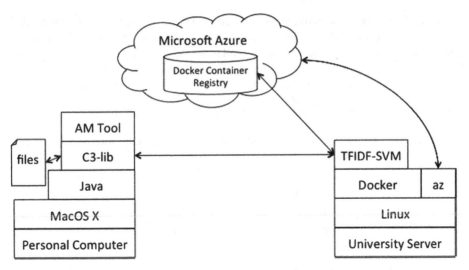

Fig. 4. Flexible setup used for experimentation.

5 Effectiveness Evaluation

5.1 General and Topic Specific Features for Argument Stance Recognition

For our original experiments in the domain of argument stance recognition, we used two different corpora of labelled arguments [6]. The first is the *annotated corpus of argumentative microtexts* (ACAM) [28]. This corpus contains 25,351 argument pairs about 795 different topics. The argument was initially intended for the argument stance same side classification task. As both arguments of every pair are individually labeled, they can be individually analyzed. This corpus is actually an amalgam of two separate corpora. The first was collected during an experiment with 23 participants discussing controversial topics in German. Their arguments were then professionally translated to English. Other argument pairs were written by Andreas Peldszus and are mainly used for teaching activities. This corpus is interesting because of the large amount of topics it covers. To further evaluate C3 we used Stab et al.'s UKP Sentential Argument Mining Corpus introduced in Sect. 2.1.

In our first experiment, we provided C3 TFIDF-SVM with all arguments from the first five topics of ACAM. These were wildly mixed, ranging from the statement that the United States policy on illegal immigration should focus on attrition through enforcement rather than amnesty to a discussion about record stores vs. internet-bought, downloaded music collections. During n-fold cross validation, the trainer service achieved 96% F1. The effectiveness to detect contra arguments was especially high with 100%. Upon inspection of the generated model, it contained terms like *violence*, *national*, or *supporters* for immigration policy or *cd*, *record*, and *collection* for the musical discussion. The second experiment was to work with larger sets of topics. We used the first 10, 20 and 40 topics of ACAM to create models in n-fold cross validation. At this point, a drawback of the TFIDF based feature extraction approach becomes apparent: The amount of features grows only slightly sub-linearly to the amount of arguments as, especially in the beginning the most representative term per document is not yet part of the automatically created controlled vocabulary. This means that the problem size for the SVM does grow almost quadratically as the dimensions as well as the amount of feature vectors grows. This drastically increases the time requirements to compute models for larger datasets and made experiments with larger datasets unfeasible on our available hardware. The results of these experiments are shown in Table 1.

Table 1. C3 TFIDF-SVM results for ACAM topic mixes using 3-fold cross validation [6].

Topic	1 to 10	1 to 20	1 to 40
Arguments	202	449	813
Terms	84	157	260
F1	88%	89%	85%

To evaluate whether the generated models generalize well, we used the model computed from the first 40 topics of ACAM to initialize an athlete service and evaluate it using a C3 committee service. The results listed in Table 2 indicate how well a model created from 5% of all available topics performs for the remaining topics.

Table 2. C3 TFIDF-SVM results for ACAM topic mixes [6].

Topic	41 to 120	41–200	41–795 (all topics)
Microaverage F1	60%	57%	57%
Microaverage precision	60%	57%	57%
Microaverage recall	60%	57%	57%
Pro F1	23%	21%	21%
Pro precision	17%	16%	15%
Pro recall	35%	34%	35%
Contra F1	73%	70%	71%
Contra precision	83%	82%	83%
Contra recall	64%	62%	62%

Similar to the previous experiments, the effectiveness to identify contra arguments is much better than that to identify pro arguments. It is noteworthy, that C3 TFIDF-SVM doesn't have the information, that both categories are mutually exclusive. Knowing the better performance of the contra category, this can easily be leveraged to increase the overall effectiveness to >70% F1. For example, only considering something a pro argument if it is identified as pro argument and simultaneously not identified as contra argument will boost the pro-category's precision to at least that of contra-category (>83% instead of >15%). Creating such informed ruled based on previous performance can be regarded as neural-symbolic integration even though TFIDF-SVM works with non-neural network based machine learning.

In all previous experiments, 3-fold cross validation was used. For another round of experimentation, we use 10-fold cross validation. As shown in Table 3, switching to 10-fold cross validation directly boosts effectiveness to >91% F1 from >85%. On the other hand applying this model to the topics >41 (similar to the experiments shown in Table 2), their effectiveness measures were reduced by up to 9%. This indicates that the 10-fold cross-validated models are over-fitted to the initial topics when compared to the models generated by 3-fold cross-validation.

Table 3. C3 TFIDF-SVM results for ACAM topic mixes using 10-fold cross validation [6].

Topic	1 to 10	1 to 20	1 to 40
Arguments	202	449	813
Terms	84	157	260
F1	95%	91%	96%

To additionally ascertain the models capability to generalize we performed multiple experiments using the UKP and transferring models between corpora. Besides creating a model from the UKP arguments using 3-fold cross validation and assessing its effectiveness, we applied the UKP model on ACAM arguments and vice versa. Table 4 contains the results of these experiments.

Table 4. C3 TFIDF-SVM results with different argument stance corpora [6].

Experiment	UKP on ACAM	UKP on UKP	ACAM on UKP
Microaverage F1	48%	60%	46%
Microaverage precision	48%	60%	46%
Microaverage recall	48%	60%	46%
Pro F1	25%	64%	25%
Pro precision	16%	62%	55%
Pro recall	52%	65%	16%
Contra F1	60%	56%	58%
Contra precision	83%	57%	44%
Contra recall	47%	55%	83%

Interestingly, whenever the ACAM corpus is involved (either as source for the model or as evaluation set) the detection of contra arguments is more effective than that of pro arguments. It is noteworthy, that the UKP corpus is inherently more difficult than the ACAM. It contains shorter arguments that are only single sentences, whereas the

ACAM contained longer debate points [6]. Compared to previous state of the art results for generalizing argument stance recognition to new topics (see Sect. 2.1), C3 TFIDF-SVM's effectiveness is 7% below that of Stab et al. with the UKP corpus. Compared to SemEval2016 challenge, our results are similar even though different datasets are used. This means that our effectiveness is comparable to that of other state of the art approaches. The key difference is that C3 TFIDF-SVM can automatically generate human readable explanations for every categorization decision and has demonstrated high generalizability as it can easily be transferred to new topics. To further investigate this transferability as well as pursuing the overall C3 goal of providing TC for any application, we used the same classifier on completely different problems. The first problem is article triage, which is the task of distinguishing relevant scientific documents from irrelevant scientific documents. The second problem is offensive language detection which we performed with a German language corpus of offensive and inoffensive tweets about politics. The third problem is intent detection for digital assistants.

5.2   Using C3 TFIDF-SVM for Article Triage

Article triage is the problem of identifying relevant articles to source arguments from. To test C3 TFIDF-SVM's utility for this task, we downloaded 200 abstracts about *melanoma* as well as 200 abstracts about *leukemia* from PubMed [1]. Both topics are types of *neoplasms* (cancers), creating a TC problem with relatively similar categories. Table 5 shows the results of the best of three models created by C3 TFIDF-SVM using 3-fold cross validation.

Table 5. TFIDF-SVM PubMed article triage results for the best model using 3-fold cross validation.

Category	Precision	Recall	F1
All microaverage	81%	81%	81%
All macroaverage	82%	78%	79%
Melanoma	85%	64%	73%
Leukemia	79%	92%	85%

As shown, the best of three models created 81% microaverage F1. The worst came up to 66% microaverage F1. Similar to Argument stance recognition, one class obtained better results than the other as leukemia related abstracts are spotted with 85% F1 while melanoma related articles are identified with 73% F1.

As this is a two-class problem, the effectiveness can again be increased by logically combining results based on known category effectiveness. The effectiveness results are comparable to those obtained in the argument stance recognition task described in Sect. 5.1. Even though the C3 API caters for hyper-parameter tuning of the training process, only our C3 TFIDF-SVM default settings have been used to create these results for a completely different TC problem. Besides the automatically generated explanations, this underlines the robustness of our approach.

5.3 Using C3 TFIDF-SVM for German Language Offensive Language Detection

To further investigate the flexibility and robustness of C3 TFIDF-SVM we switched natural languages and applied it to German language offensive language detection. The GermEval 2018 Shared Task on the Identification of Offensive Language aims at the identification of offensive language in German Twitter tweets [29]. It contains a training set consisting out of 5,009 tweets. 1,778 of these contain offensive language. It additionally contains a test set of 3,532 tweets, 1,202 of which are offensive. We created a TFIDF-SVM model using the training set and evaluated in on the test set using the C3 committee service. Table 6 contains the results of this experiment.

Table 6. C3 TFIDF-SVM GermEval 2018 results using its default configuration.

Category	Precision	Recall	F1
All microaverage	60%	60%	60%
All macroaverage	56%	56%	56%
Other	70%	70%	70%
Offensive	41%	40%	41%

The results are similar to those obtained for the argument stance recognition task. In this case, the identification of non-offensive language was more effective than that of offensive language. The original GermEval 2018 competition had 51 entries. C3 TFIDF-SVM has not participated. If it had, it would have been on place 42. Notably, the creation of the model during n-fold cross validation has shown, that the detection of the OTHER category was possible with more than twice the F1 as the detection of offensive language. As C3 TFIDF-SVM is not aware of this mutual exclusiveness, a simple logical rule to only take OTHER results into account would improve C3 TFIDF-SVM's effectiveness to 70%. The winner of GermEval 2018 used a complicated committee of multiple classifiers along with manually crafted lexicons of offensive language to obtain 77% F1.

This shows, that C3 TFIDF-SVM can be used in different natural languages with minimal manual effort. The generated results are close to that of competition winners while automated human readable explanations are generated. These explanations can subsequently be taken into account when creating lexica for offensive language identification.

5.4 Using C3 TFIDF-SVM for Digital Assistant Intent Detection

A primary task for digital assistants or chat bots is intent recognition: The detection of the task that should be performed by the system [30]. This is a TC problem with more than two categories. To evaluate C3 TFIDF-SVM on this problem, we used the benchmark for digital assistants created by Coucke et al. [30]. The actual benchmark focuses on named-entity recognition within text. Therefore the benchmark contains the original text as well as one that is annotated with relevant named entities. This allows us two experiments: The first is to test TFIDF-SVM with the normal texts. The second is to replace certain text parts with the detected entity in preprocessing and evaluating C3

TFIDF-SVM with these augmented texts. Coucke et al.'s benchmark has seven different categories and is already split in a test and evaluation set. There are 400 training samples and 100 evaluation samples per category. Table 7 shows the results of a model tested by the C3 committee service.

Table 7. C3 TFIDF-SVM evaluation set results for intent detection without decoding named entities.

Category	Precision	Recall	F1
All microaverage	73%	57%	64%
All macroaverage	72%	57%	64%
Add to playlist	73%	27%	39%
Book restaurant	79%	69%	74%
Get weather	78%	54%	64%
Play music	60%	48%	53%
Rate book	82%	89%	85%
Search creative work	52%	32%	40%
Search screening event	80%	78%	79%

Even though the individual results differ from those obtained during the 3-fold cross validation process of the original model, the microaverage F1 is in both cases 64%. This highlights the robustness of C3 TFIDF-SVM's models when transferred to previously unseen data. For the next experiment, named entities were decoded. This means that for instance strings like *música libre* were replaced by their common entity *playlist*. The n-fold cross validation process using TFIDF-SVM's default settings created almost perfect results on the training set with these augmentations with 98% microaverage F1. These values were reduced down to 89% microaverage F1 when the model was evaluated with the evaluation set as shown in Table 8:

Table 8. C3 TFIDF-SVM evaluation set results for intent detection with decoded named entities.

Category	Precision	Recall	F1
All microaverage	81%	98%	89%
All macroaverage	81%	99%	89%
Add to playlist	91%	100%	95%
Book restaurant	82%	94%	88%
Get weather	81%	100%	89%
Play music	76%	99%	86%
Rate book	83%	100%	90%
Search creative work	76%	99%	86%
Search screening event	82%	98%	89%

These results show that C3 TFIDF-SVM can be combined with a preprocessing step to identify relevant named entities which strongly increase effectiveness. They also show that the system is able to generalize to different problems with more categories.

6   Understandability Survey

Different from most state of the art classifiers, C3 TFIDF-SVM generates human readable explanations for its generated results and the generated models can easily be manually inspected. The pattern to generate explanations is slightly updated from that described in the beginning of Sect. 3 to cater for more TC problems than argument stance recognition. In order to measure how well average people understand and explanation we performed a survey for which we got 26 replies. All survey participants were native German speakers. Because the generated explanations were in English, some potential participants refused to participate because the level of English in the survey was too challenging for them. About 75% of actual participants have a university degree. About 80% of the participants work in the field of information technology and computer science albeit some work in supporting functions like sales, accounting and marketing. As we deemed it the most relatable problem, we chose the explanation for the digital assistant intent detection experiment described in Sect. 5.4. C3 TFIDF-SVM was confronted with the message *"I'd like to have this track onto my Classical Relaxations playlist."* It correctly assigned it to the category *add to playlist* with and without decoded named entities.

First, the participants were asked to state if they understand the following explanation: *"This document is considered to belong to category "Add to Playlist", because it contains occurrences of the terms* classical, have, d. *In 2100 previously analyzed documents, the occurrence of these terms in their relative amounts indicated a 99.97% probability for a document to belong to category "Add to Playlist". The likelihood has to be at least 10% to be assigned to this category."*

19 out of 26 participants understood the explanation. TFIDF-SVM removes special characters during tokenization. Therefore *I'd* becomes two individual words *I* and *d*. This created a lot of confusion under the participants, many of whom stated that there is no *d* in the sentence so they suspected some kind of error.

Second, the participants were confronted with the automatically generated explanation for the case of decoded named entities. The explanation was as follows: *"This document is considered to belong to category "Add to Playlist", because it contains occurrences of the terms playlist, add, item, music. In 2100 previously analyzed documents, the occurrence of these terms in their relative amounts indicated a 99.99% probability for a document to belong to category "Add to Playlist". The likelihood has to be at least 10% to be assigned to this category."*

23 out of 26 participants understood this explanation which is a significant increase to that without decoding named entities. Interestingly, only one participant noticed, that the words *add*, *item* and *music* do not literally occur within the sentence while many pointed out, that there is no single *d* in the first explanation. This survey gave us two insights: Firstly, the automatically generated explanations are understandable by the majority of survey participants that speak the language the explanation is in. Secondly, more abstract concepts such as *item* and *music* were better understandable by survey participants.

7 Conclusions

7.1 About Topic Specific and General Terms as Features

Between our argument stance recognition experiments with the ACAM corpus we manually inspected the model's controlled vocabulary for every learned topic. This was feasible for the first 40 topics as the model contained 260 terms. C3 TFIDF-SVM identified over 1000 terms for UKP which made manual inspection unfeasible. Besides many topic specific terms, the model also contained general terms such as *incredibly, uncomfortable, radical, death, stress, knowledge, greedy, tragedy, concern, racist, cruel, presents, reason, justice, pleasure,* and *punishment.* These general terms oftentimes carry a specific sentiment. Especially the negative sentiment is more easily identifiable. In our opinion, this is the reason why the recognition of contra arguments outperformed that of pro arguments when ACAM is involved (see Sect. 5.1).

In combination with our experimental results, these terms support our hypothesis of general and topic specific argument stance features. During evaluations of the classifier with known topics, higher effectiveness results were observed than during to previously unknown topics (>85% F1 for ACAM and >60% F1 for UKP compared to >57% F1 for ACAM and >46% F1 for UKP).

Argument specificity and therefore the intersections of $F(n)$ and $F(m)$ for topics n and m can be seen as flexible because certain terms can have completely different meanings in other topics or the topics have overlapping concerns. The machine learned hyperplanes of C3 TFIDF-SVM models should compensate this by being under or above most values for this dimension. An example for such a term is *drug* which can have an entirely different meaning in the context of medical treatment and policies on drug abuse. To further test this thesis, we created new models on other topic blocks of ACAM (41–80, 81–120, and 121–160). Evaluating these models with the remaining topics of ACAM created similarly effective results than those shown in Table 2. Manual inspection of these generated models shows that they contain many more general terms like *local, prisoners, test, information, money, team, death, love, workers, women, rights, knowledge, child, gifts, unhealthy, exists, over, uncomfortable, power, students,* and *war.* It also contains some words indicating who is referring to what like *my, I, he, your,* or *she.* Some of the terms seem to be specific to more than one topic. Like the afore mentioned *drugs* or the term *marriage* which can be seen as literal or proverbial.

To provide further examples for such topic specificity, we manually assessed 400 explanations that were created by C3 TFIDF-SVM when using a model trained on the first 40 ACAM topics and tasking it with the categorization of explanations from ACAM topics 41–80. One such explanation is: *"This document is considered to belong to category "Pro", because it contains occurrences of the terms* mechanism, enough, your, cruel. *In 814 previously analyzed documents, the occurrence of these terms in their relative amounts indicated a 99.79% probability for a document to belong to category "Pro". The likelihood has to be at least 50% to be assigned to this category."*

We listed the identified features in Table 9 which differentiates them by which type of explanations they occurred in. The explanations can either be for correct or incorrect categorizations for the categories *Pro* and *Contra.*

Table 9. Specific features from ACAM explanations. The listed terms occurred in pro and contra explanations for categorizations that are either correct or incorrect.

Categorization types in which explanations terms occurred	Terms
All categorization types	Always, day, emissions, enough, governments, he, I, money, my, reason, scheme, united, your
Correct Pro categorizations	Christmas, collection, concern, condemnation, cruel, document, earth, football, heart, marriage, numerous, punishment, quote, regular, scots, St, suffer, test, treatment, truth, Wikileaks, women
All Pro categorizations but not in Contra categorizations	Age, Britain, child, economy, knowledge, report, school, single
Incorrect Pro categorizations	Added, bishop, immigrants, immigration, paying, renewable, represents, richest, round, speed, suffer, tab, workers
Correct Contra categorizations	Anne, applications, improvement, injury, looked, points, positive, relies, signature, soldiers, station
All Contra categorizations but not in Pro categorizations	Anger, exactly, fans, Korea, love, racist
Incorrect Contra categorizations	Deaths, justice, pleasure, stopped, stress, unemployment
Occurring in different categorization types	British, children, claim, compared, crisis, death, EU, Europe, experience, food, games, greedy, information, mechanisms, ideas, information, nations, north, music, mp, Obama, over, powers, president, prisoners, rights, soldiers, she, want, water

Because the text categorization uses SVMs, the combination of relative itfidf values for these terms determines whether an argument is categorized as pro or contra. This analysis still yielded some interesting insights for useful features. For instance, features that only occurred in the explanations for incorrect categorizations are likely to be topic specific for ACAM topics 1–40 but not 41–80. Two examples for such feature terms are the terms *added* and *immigrants* that only occurred in the explanations of incorrect categorizations of ACAM topics 41–80 but occurred in the explanations of correct categorizations for ACAM topics 1–40.

7.2 About Flexible, Explainable and Robust Text Categorization

Our contribution is four-fold: We firstly developed a robust text categorization classifier that can be used for argument stance recognition and achieves reasonable results for previously unseen topics. This way, it can be used directly to identify the argument stances during the construction of the RecomRatio argument ontology. It also serves as basis for creating an ontology of argument stance features based on the generated explanations per argument.

We secondly proposed our thesis of general and topic specific features which is supported by our experiments. These can be used to structure known argument stance features as shown in Fig. 3. Such ontologies can form a basis to implement explanation support for other non-semantic applications. If individual concepts that were found as argument stance features are represented by more general hyper concepts, these could additionally be used as features for specific stances.

Our third contribution is the short development time needed to provide an application with machine learning based text categorization. The development work necessary to perform the experiments described in Sects. 5.2, 5.3 and 5.4 only consisted of data engineering to import the labeled data to C3's interface. It was below 2 h for all implementations. Neural-symbolic integrated applications are easy to develop if one only has to focus on the symbolic part as the machine learning based aspect is encapsulated behind an easy to use API that does not require any hyper-parameter tuning to produce useful results. C3 TFIDF-SVM is not only easily transferrable to new topics in the argument stance recognition problem but can also be applied to any TC problem where reasonable results can be achieved without hyper-parameter tuning.

Our fourth contribution is our work in automatically explainable explanations. The proposed approach requires no additional manually created resources besides appropriately labelled texts to create human readable explanations why certain categorizations were performed. These explanations are understood by the majority of survey participants. This makes C3 TFIDF-SVM safe to use for any enterprise grade application which has to cope with the regulatory requirement of providing explanations for the results of their applications.

Acknowledgements. This work has been funded by the Deutsche Forschungsgemeinschaft (DFG) within the project Empfehlungsrationalisierung, Grant Number 376059226, as part of the Priority Program "Robust Argumentation Machines (RATIO)" (SPP-1999).

References

1. US National Library of Medicine National Institutes of Health pubmed.gov. https://www.ncbi.nlm.nih.gov/pubmed/. Accessed 17 Sep 2019
2. European Parliament and of the Council of 27 April 2016 on the protection of natural persons with regard to the processing of personal data and on the free movement of such data, and repealing Directive 95/46/EC (General Data Protection Regulation) (Text with EEA relevance); OJ L, 4 May, 2016, vol. 119, pp. 1–88 (2016)
3. Clos, J., Wiratunga, N., Massie, S.: Towards explainable text classification by jointly learning lexicon and modifier terms. In: IJCAI-17 Workshop on Explainable AI (XAI) (2017)
4. Lippi, M., Torroni, P.: Argument mining: a machine learning perspective. In: Black, E., Modgil, S., Oren, N. (eds.) TAFA 2015. LNCS (LNAI), vol. 9524, pp. 163–176. Springer, Cham (2015). https://doi.org/10.1007/978-3-319-28460-6_10

5. Mohammad, S., Kiritchenko, S., Sobhani, P., Zhu, X., Cherry, C: Semeval-2016 task 6: detecting stance in tweets. In: Proceedings of the 10th International Workshop on Semantic Evaluation (SemEval-2016), pp. 31–41 (2016)
6. Eljasik-Swoboda, T., Engel, F., Hemmje, M.: Using topic specific features for argument stance recognition. In: Proceedings of the 8th International Conference on Data Science, Technology and Applications (DATA 2019), pp. 13–22 (2019). ISBN:978-989-758-377-3
7. Mohammad, S.M., Sobhani, P., Kiritchenko, S.: Stance and sentiment in tweets. ACM Trans. Internet Technol. Argument. Soc. Media **17**, 1–23 (2016)
8. Stab, C., Miller, T., Schiller, B., Rai, P., Gurevych, I.: Cross-topic argument mining from heterogeneous sources. In: Proceedings of the Conference on Empirical Methods in Natural Language Processing (EMNLP 2018) (2018)
9. Same Side Stance Classification. https://sameside.webis.de/. Accessed 24 Sep 2019
10. Sebastiani, F.: Machine learning in automated text categorization. ACM Comput. Surv. **34**, 1–47 (2002)
11. Bader, S., Hitzler, P.: Dimensions of neural-symbolic integration – a structured survey. arXiv preprint arXiv:cs/0511042 (2005)
12. Swoboda, T., Kaufmann, M., Hemmje, M.: Toward cloud-based classification and annotation support. In: Proceedings of the 6th International Conference on Cloud Computing and Services Science (CLOSER 2016), vol. 2, pp. 131–237 (2016)
13. McCulloch, W.S., Pitts, W.: A logical calculus of the ideas immanent in nervous activity. Bull. Math. Biophys. **5**, 115–133 (1943)
14. Helbig, H., Scherer, A.: Kurs 1830: Neuronale Netze. University of Hagen, Germany (2011)
15. Arel, I., Rose, D.C., Karnowski, T.P.: Deep machine learning – a new frontier in artificial intelligence research. In: IEEE Computational Intelligence Magazine, USA, November issue, pp. 13–18 (2010)
16. Vapnik, V.N., Chervonenkis, A.Y.: On a class of algorithms of learning pattern recognition. Framework of the Generalised Portrait Method, Об одном классе алгоритмов обучения распознаванию образов, Автоматика и телемеханика (1964)
17. Chang, C., Lin, C.: LIBSVM: a library for support vector machines. ACM Trans. Intell. Syst. Technol. **2**(3), 1–27 (2011)
18. Mikolov, T., Chen, K., Corrado, G., Dean, J.: Efficient estimation of word representation in vector space. In: Proceedings of Workshop at ICLR (2013)
19. Pennington, J., Socher, R., Manning, C.: GloBe: global vectors for word representation. In: Empirical Methods in Natural Language Processing, pp. 1532–1543 (2014)
20. Zanzotto, F.M., Korkontzelos, I., Fallucchi, F., Manandhar, S.: Estimating linear models for compositional distributed semantics. In: Proceedings of the 23rd International Conference on Computational Linguistics, pp. 1263–1271 (2010)
21. Kusner, M.J., Sun, Y., Kolkin, N., Weinberger, K.Q.: From word embeddings to document distances. In: Proceedings of the 32nd International Conference on Machine Learning (2015)
22. Dai, X., Bikdash, M., Meyer, M.: From social media to public health surveillance: word embedding based clustering method for twitter classification. In: Proceedings of SoutheastCon, pp. 1–7 (2017). https://doi.org/10.1109/secon.2017.7925400
23. Eljasik-Swoboda, T., Kaufmann, M., Hemmje, M.: No target function classifier – fast unsupervised text categorization using semantic spaces. In: Proceedings of the 7th International Conference on Data Science, Technology and Applications (DATA 2018), pp. 35–46 (2018)
24. Devlin, J., Chang, M.W., Lee, K., Toutanova, K.: BERT: pre-training of deep bidirectional transformers for language understanding. arXiv:1810.04805v2 (2019)
25. Wolff, E.: Microservices – Flexible Software Architecture. Pearson Education, USA (2017)
26. Dropwizard: Production-ready, out of the box. https://dropwizard.io. Accessed 12 Sep 2019
27. Enterprise Container Platform | Docker. https://www.docker.com/. Accessed 30 Sep 2019

28. Peldszus, A.: An annotated corpus of argumentative microtexts. https://github.com/peldszus/arg-microtexts. Accessed 15 Mar 2019
29. Wiegand, M., Siegel, M., Ruppenhofer, J.: Overview of the GermEval 2018 shared task on the identification of offensive language. In: Proceedings of the GermEval, Vienna, Austria (2018)
30. Coucke, A., et al.: Snipts voice platform, an embedded spoken language understanding system for private-by-design voice interfaces. arXiv:1805.10190 (2018)

Dealing with Critical Issues in Emails: A Comparison of Approaches for Sentiment Analysis

Bernd Markscheffel$^{(\boxtimes)}$ ⓘ and Markus Haberzettl

Department of Information and Knowledge Management, Technische Universität Ilmenau,
Ilmenau, Germany
{bernd.markscheffel,markus.haberzettl}@tu-ilmenau.de

Abstract. The customer service of larger companies is constantly faced with the challenge of mastering the daily flood of incoming emails. In particular, the effort involved in dealing with critical issues, such as complaints, and the insufficient resources available to deal with them can have a negative impact on customer relations and thus on the public perception of companies. It is therefore necessary to assess and prioritise these concerns automatically, if possible. It is therefore necessary to evaluate and prioritise these concerns automatically if possible. The sentiment analysis as the automatic recognition of the sentiment in texts enables such prioritisation. The sentiment analysis of German-language e-mails is still an open research problem and till now there is no evidence of a dominant approach in this field. The aim of this article is to compare three approaches for the sentiment analysis of German emails:

The first approach (A) is based on the combination of sentiment lexicons and machine learning methods. The second (B) is the extension of approach A by further feature extraction methods and the third approach (C) is a deep learning approach based on the combination of Word Embeddings and Convolutional Neural Networks (CNN). A gold standard corpus is generated to compare these approaches. Based on this corpus, systematic experiments are carried out in which the different method combinations for the approaches are examined.

The results of the experiments show that the Deep Learning approach is more effective than classical approaches and generates better classification results.

Keywords: Sentiment analysis · Machine learning · Feature extraction methods · Deep learning · KNIME

1 Introduction

1.1 Problem Description

Only 127 years have elapsed between Samuel Morse's milestone in the history of communication systems when he sent the Bible quote "What hath God wrought?" and Ray Tomlinson's keyboard line "QWERTYUIOP" as content of the first email. Meanwhile emails

© Springer Nature Switzerland AG 2020
S. Hammoudi et al. (Eds.): DATA 2019, CCIS 1255, pp. 23–36, 2020.
https://doi.org/10.1007/978-3-030-54595-6_2

are not to be dismissed from the daily life any longer, even more, enterprises see in emails the preferential communication channel in particular for customer service [1, 2]. The increasing amount of emails arriving daily at customer service poses a challenge for the prompt processing of customer concerns in companies [2]. Automated prioritization is necessary in order to identify and prioritize critical concerns to avoid the risk of negative effects on the perception of companies. One form of prioritization is the sentiment, the emotionally annotated mood and opinion in an email [3]. A sentiment is also an approach to solving further problems such as the analysis of the course of customer contacts, email marketing or the identification of critical topics [4]. Linguistic data processing (LDV) approaches are used to automatically capture sentiment [5].

Although the number of published research papers is increasing, sentiment analysis continues to be an open research problem [6, 7]. In especial view, there is a lack of in approaches specifically for the German language, whereby the automated classification of polarity in the categories positive, negative and neutral is of particular interest [8–10]. In research, methods of machine learning have prevailed over knowledge- and dictionary-based methods to determine polarity [8]. The reason for this is that machine learning methods approach human accuracy and are not restricted by the other two approaches (e.g. lack of dynamics in relation to informal language) [11, 12]. Knowledge- and dictionary-based methods define the rules manually. In contrast to that, machine learning represents the fully automated inductive detection of such rules using algorithms developed for this purpose [12]. So far, no machine learning method or procedures and approaches based on it have been identified as dominant - another reason why sentiment analysis is today still an open research problem [3, 5, 13].

1.2 Research Questions

There are several solutions for this problem. One approach for the classification of polarity is seen in the combination of sentiment dictionaries and machine learning methods [14] – experiment A. Further potential is considered in the combination of such lexicons and learning methods with other methods of feature extraction – experiment B. This paper is a significant extension of our previous conference paper [27] where we have discussed only these two approaches as a hybrid of classical methods. Stojanowski et al. [15] see the Deep Learning approach in the context of sentiment analysis through the automation of feature extraction as more robust and flexible than the classical procedures mentioned above, especially when used in different domains (language, text structure) – our experiment C.

The main aim of this paper is to compare these approaches for German-language emails at the document level. We will answer the questions: do machine learning methods based on sentiment lexicons generate better results in the context of sentiment analysis if the lexicon is combined with other methods of feature extraction and how does a Deep Learning solution based on the combination of Word Embeddings and CNN compare to the results of experiments A and B. The paper is structured as follows. Section 2 describes the methodology of our research, Sect. 3 presents and compares the results of our several experiments before we summarize and give an outlook on future work in Sect. 4.

2 Methodology

2.1 Literature Analysis and Related Work

The several machine learning and feature extraction methods to be identified for the different approaches are determined by a systematic literature analysis according to Webster and Watson [16]) and is additionally supplemented by Prabowo and Thelwall [17] when structuring the findings. The complete methodology and the results of the literature analysis, the determined machine learning methods, the identified relevant feature extraction methods and a comprehensive presentation of related work are described by Haberzettl and Markscheffel [18].

2.2 Implementation

We have implemented these to be compared approaches with the Konstanz Information Miner (KNIME) in version 3.5.2.25. The data required for implementation are acquired according to the Gold Standard requirements of Wissler et al. (2014). The results of the approaches will then be compared using identified quality criteria, which have been recognized in the context.

2.3 Data Acquisition

Text data are unstructured data. For the real classification, process it is necessary convert it into structured data. This data is collected in a corpus and split into a training - and a test data set for the analysis process. As no suitable, freely accessible corpus is available for this task, a separate corpus must be created and coded that meets the requirements of the Gold Standard.

For this purpose, 7,000 requests from private customers to the customer service of a company in the telecommunication sector are used. Since a full survey is not possible due to the manual coding effort and no information on the distribution of polarity in the population is available, this sample was determined based on a simple random selection. Coding by only one expert should be rejected, especially in view of the Gold Standard requirements. The argumentation for a higher data consistency due to this is to be critically considered especially in light of the subjectivity of the sentiment, because sentiment is interpreted differently by different persons, for example, due to different life experiences [4, 19, 20]. This characteristic has to be reflected in the corpus. The following parameters, therefore, apply to the coding: Emails should be evaluated from the writer's point of view and categorized exclusively as an entire document. In addition, only subjective statements are relevant for determining positive or negative sentiments. The coding was therefore carried out in three steps:

1. The sample was divided into seven equally sized data sets. These sets were coded by six different experts who had previously received a codebook with instructions (the assignment of the groups was random in each phase; no reviewer coded a document twice). In addition to the general conditions, the codebook contains the class scale to be used and instructions for the classification of the classes (1 – very positive ...5 – very negative and 6 – Mixed, which contains positive and negative elements).

2. The sets were again coded by different experts due to the subjective interpretation of the sentiment. This expert had no information about the previous coding.
3. All emails were identified, which were coded differently in each of the previous steps. These emails were assigned to a new expert for the set, who performed a third encoding.

After coding, the corpus is divided into a training and test data set in a stratified manner with a ratio of 70:30. Then the emails are converted into documents.

2.4   Data Preprocessing

The emails are already pre-processed in the source system:

– Personal customer data (name, address, etc.) have been anonymized and replaced.
– HTML tags, meta data (sender, IDs, etc.), attachments have been deleted and
– Message histories in the emails are removed.

Nevertheless, there is a large number of non-text elements to be found and have to be eliminated. The pre-processing workflow consists of the following steps:

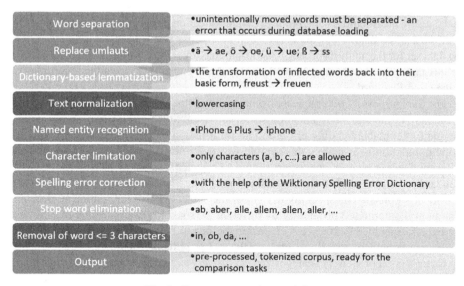

Fig. 1. Data preprocessing workflow

2.5   Feature Extraction and Selection

In a next step, we have to extract features from this corpus. Features are defined as numerically measurable attributes and properties of data. In the context of text mining, feature extraction should be understood as the *structuring process of unstructured data.* The extraction is split into two parts: Features are generated on the one hand by direct conversion of texts or tokens and on the other hand by applying the feature extracting methods identified and introduced by Haberzettl, and Markscheffel [18]. Table 1 collects the several feature extraction methods used in our approach.

Table 1. Feature extraction methods [18]

n-Gramm	n-G
Term frequency - Inverse document frequency	TF-IDF
Term presence	TP
Term frequency	TF
Part of speech tagging	POS
Modification feature	MF
Negation	NEG
Pointwise Mutual Information (PMI)	PMI
Sentiment Dictionary (SM)	SM
Category (Cat)	CAT
Corpus specific	COR

2.6   Sentiment Lexicon

Sentiment dictionaries are dictionaries in which words are assigned to a polarity index. Sentiment dictionaries are context-sensitive, i.e. words and values contained in them apply primarily to the context in which they were created. Since no suitable dictionary exists for the context of German-language emails, such a dictionary had to be created. For resource reasons, an automated, corpus-based approach was pursued.

According to SentiWS [21] a generation on co-occurrence based rules is chosen. Pointwise Mutual Information (PMI) is used as a method for the analysis of co-occurrence and thus for the determination of semantic orientation [21–23]. In our specific case, two million uncoded emails were acquired from the same database as the corpus. Random sampling made the selection. All emails were pre-processed according to the process described in Fig. 1. For all words contained in these emails the semantic orientation {positive, negative} was determined on the basis of the PMI [21, 22], i.e. for each word its similarity to previously defined positive or negative seed words is calculated. For each of the 93,170 words identified, a threshold value for clipping the lexicon SO-PMI $\in [-0,13; 0,08]$ was determined by manual checking, taking into account the Zipf-distribution, so that the final lexicon consists of 1,704 negative and 955 positive words. Table 2 shows a cut-out of the sentiment dictionary with its top ten positive and negative normalized PMI-values, whereby the normalization is within the boundaries $-1 < PMI < 1$.

Table 2. Cut-out of the sentiment dictionary SentiMail (SM) [27].

Positive term	Scaled PMI	Negative term	Scaled PMI
herzlich	1	betruegen	−1
empathisch	0,9786	verarschen	−0,983
beglueckwuenschen	0,9589	andrehen	−0,9798
angenehm	0,954	dermassen	−0,9743
bedanken	0,9259	vertrauensbruch	−0,9628
kompliment	0,9156	scheiss	−0,9336
danke	0,9148	anluegen	−0,9263
sympathischen	0,9134	abzocke	−0,9233
sympathisch	0,8956	taeuschung	−0,9181
nervositaet	0,878	geschaeftsgebaren	−0,9137

3 Experiments and Results

For experiment A and B various machine learning methods were identified and introduced by Haberzettl, and Markscheffel [18, 27]. In Table 3 we have collected the several identified machine-learning methods used in approach A and B.

Table 3. Machine-learning methods used in experiment A and B [18, 27].

Support Vector Machine	SVM
Artificial Neural Network	ANN
Naive Bayes	NB
Logistic Regression or Maximum Entropy	LR or ME
k-nN nearest neighbor	k-nN

The implementation of the machine-learning methods in combination with the above introduced feature extracting methods was done with different libraries of Weka integration of KNIME (e.g. LibSVM, NaiveBayesMultinominal) or it could directly implemented as nodes (LR Logistics (3, 7), k-nN). The ANN was realized by a multi-layer perceptron starting from our multi-class case. A layer and M/2 (M = feature) neurons in this layer were chosen as a starting point and then successively increased to M + 2 neurons.

3.1 Evaluation

The results of the experiments and thus the classification itself are to be evaluated with the use of quality criteria. With the help of a confusion matrix, the results of the classification can be divided according to positive and negative cases. The four resulting cases from the classification in the confusion matrix (true positive, true negative, false positive, false negative) allow the derivation of the following different quality criteria: Accuracy (ACC), Precision (PRE), Recall (REC) and F-Measure (F1) [24, 25]. The validity of the quality criteria is ensured by a 10-fold stratified cross-validation [26]. Accuracy is used as the decisive criterion for determining the best result due to the limitations discussed by Haberzettl, and Markscheffel in [18, 27].

3.2 Experiments and Results for the Sentiment Dictionary (A) and Feature Extraction (B)

In a first step, based on the approaches A and B, the sentiment lexicon to be used was first determined. For this purpose, all learning methods were trained on the features of the two used lexicons (SentiWS [21] and SentiMail-SM, see Sect. 2.6) and the combination of both. The result is the result of experiment A. Figure 2 shows the corresponding workflow implemented with KNIME for experiments A and B [27].

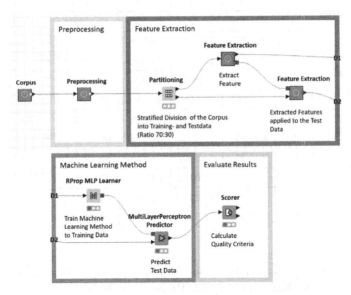

Fig. 2. KNIME workflow for the experiments A and B [27].

The results of the first experiment are obvious (see Table 4): For each learning method, the combination of both sentiment lexicons is the best alternative with regard to each quality criterion. Only the precision at NB is better with SentiWS - probably, measured by the recall, due to the simple assignment of the emails to the most frequented class (neutral). Particularly, with regard to the exactness (Precision, Recall, F1-Measure), the combination of both lexicon is dominant [27]. Table 4 shows a compilation of the results.

So, out of the results of experiment A both sentiment lexicon were selected from the results of A. It should be noted that the SentiMail (SM) lexicon, created within the context, produces better results in direct comparison with SentiWS (SW) - this substantiates the need for context-dependent sentiment dictionaries. The rank assigned according to Accuracy indicates that the best result for experiment A is the combination of ANN and both sentiment dictionaries. This result is also confirmed by the remaining quality criteria (F1 is to be weighted higher than the Precision outlier is) [27].

Table 4. Comparison of the sentiment lexicons SentiMail (SM) and SentiWS (SW) as feature extraction method and the best result (R), evaluated according to accuracy for approach A [27].

	R	ACC	PRE	REC	F1	
SVM	2	83,19%	83,26%	71,43%	75,87%	SMSW
	5	80,41%	80,18%	63,76%	69,14%	SM
	9	78,44%	74,70%	62,25%	65,86%	SM
ANN	1	83,82%	82,26%	74,55%	77,78%	SMSW
	4	81,44%	79,68%	68,20%	72,49%	SM
	7	79,17%	73,64%	65,98%	68,83%	SM
NB	12	75,67%	68,47%	67,81%	67,16%	SMSW
	14	74,47%	67,45%	63,95%	63,92%	SM
	15	72,89%	71,59%	47,41%	49,75%	SM
ME	3	82,73%	82,22%	70,97%	75,21%	SMSW
	6	80,33%	79,35%	64,22%	69,32%	SM
	10	78,32%	74,30%	61,74%	65,72%	SM
KnN	8	79,14%	75,01%	69,23%	71,65%	SMSW
	11	77,58%	71,81%	65,75%	68,22%	SM
	13	75,09%	67,88%	61,70%	64,08%	SM

For the second experiment (B), the best lexicon for each learning method is used. In the following step, we had to determine which frequency is to be used for the unigrams. The background for this is the often cited comparison between term presence (TP) and relative term frequency (relTF), at which the term presence dominates [28]. For this purpose, each machine learning method was trained with all three-frequency types (TP, relTF, TF-IDF) in each case as well as the identified sentiment lexicons from the previous experiment step. Only the frequency, which achieves the best results according to Accuracy, was selected for each learning method. The results of the remaining 62 possible combinations of the feature categories for each learning method are evaluated, whereby each of these combinations must inevitably contain the sentiment dictionary and produces the results for experiment B, (see Table 5) [27].

Table 5. Comparison of term presence (TP) vs. TF-IDF vs. relative term frequency (relTF) as additional features for approach A = experiment B [27]

	R	ACC	PRE	REC	F1	
SVM	1	84,67%	80,93%	76,65%	78,59%	TP
	2	84,16%	84,38%	73,48%	77,73%	TF-IDF
	3	83,73%	83,99%	72,55%	76,93%	Rel TF
ANN	7	77,02%	67,17%	67,01%	67,06%	TP
	8	76,92%	67,40%	65,98%	66,65%	TF-IDF
	9	75,72%	65,48%	66,39%	65,91%	Rel TF
NB	4	81,32%	74,08%	78,26%	75,96%	TP
	5	78,83%	71,86%	72,95%	72,23%	TF-IDF
	6	77,87%	71,15%	70,51%	70,56%	Rel TF
ME	10	72,83%	61,79%	67,14%	63,75%	TP
	12	71,33%	59,98%	64,51%	61,77%	TF-IDF
	13	71,30%	60,04%	64,86%	61,91%	Rel TF
KnN	11	72,43%	70,51%	52,80%	51,34%	TP
	14	69,29%	58,60%	59,01%	54,93%	Rel TF
	15	68,28%	56,88%	60,59%	55,05%	TF-IDF

Table 5 illustrates that the values for term presence (TP) are better than the values for TF-IDF as well as to the relative term frequency (relTF). So, only term presence for unigrams was used for all machine learning methods. The accuracy of the previously best learning method (ANN) decreases by 6.8% points, while, for example, the accuracy of the SVM (F1-Measure) increases further. This mainly reflects the core characteristics of the SVM, which benefits significantly more from large feature vectors than other learning methods. Also noteworthy is the small difference between TF-IDF and relTF. Although four of the five learning methods achieved a higher accuracy with TF-IDF than with the relative term frequency, the results of the quality criteria between the two frequencies usually deviate only marginally. As Table 6 shows, the results of SVM as well as of NB and ME with approach B are significantly better with regard to Accuracy and F1-Measure than in approach A. In particular, the 6.6% points higher accuracy and the 9.78% points higher F1 measurement at NB should be highlighted. ANN and k-nN show no significant deviations from A, whereby the ANN generates marginally worse results with respect to almost all quality criteria than in approach A [27].

Table 6. Best results for experiment B (R measured by accuracy), i.e. for features in combination with SentiWS and SentiMail [27].

	R	ACC	PRE	REC	F1	
SVM	1	85,03%	81,22%	77,98%	79,49%	POS, Neg, n-G
ANN	2	83,64%	81,84%	74,79%	77,83%	TF
NB	4	82,27%	75,62%	78,44%	76,94%	POS, Booster, Neg, n-G
ME	3	83,28%	81,43%	72,52%	76,14%	TF, POS, Cat
KnN	5	79,95%	77,22%	68,26%	71,77%	TF

3.3 Experiments and Results for the Deep Learning Approach as a Combination of Word Embeddings and CNN (C)

As described above, Stojanovski et al. [15] see the advantage of deep learning in the context of sentiment analysis in automated feature extraction. Here they refer to the connection of Word Embeddings and Convolutional Neural Networks (CNN). This approach is our role model for Experiment C.

Word embeddings represent words or tokens as vectors which, together with the inherent syntactic and semantic information, make it possible to assign these words to certain contexts [28–30]. To generate this information or to determine the vectors, there are different procedures. One of the most popular is the Word2Vec model according to Mikolov et al. [30]. Stojanovski et al. [15] also use Word2Vec, which is why we have also chosen it for our Deep Learning approach C. Word2Vec contains two methods for calculating Word embeddings: Continuous Bag of Words (CBOW) and Skip-gram [31]. The generated word vectors serve as input for the CNN. Additionally, due to the context of document classification, the approach presented by Le and Mikolov [32] is used to apply Word2Vec to Doc2Vec documents. Doc2Vec creates an n-dimensional document representation instead of the previous word representation. The vector calculation principles analogous to Word2Vec are Distributed Memory (DM) and Distributed Bag of Words (DBOW) [31] in the Doc2Vec context. In our approach, the Deeplearning4java (DL4J) integration in KNIME is used for the calculation of Word embeddings and Doc2Vec vectors. CBOW and Skip Gram are applied to the 2 million data sets already used for the creation of the sentiment lexicon. While the word relations were generated unsupervised, DBOW and DM allow the monitored generation on the training data. In this case, the tag of the documents has to be replaced by the respective class of the document. Thus, Doc2Vec makes it possible to calculate the relationships of words in the context of the sentiment of the document.

For the comparison of the results, the contextually unrelated Word Embeddings pre-trained by Reimers et al. [33] are used. The training parameters correspond to the findings of Mikolov et al. [31], where the word or Doc2Vec vector length is n = 300. The architecture of CNN is based on Stojanovski et al. in the given context. The implementation of the CNN takes place by means of the Keras implementation in KNIME.

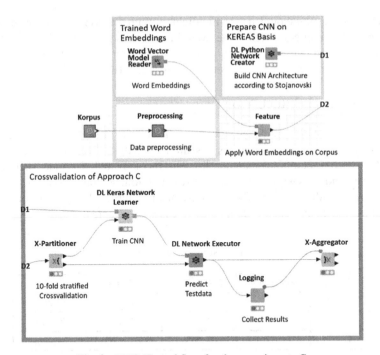

Fig. 3. KNIME workflow for the experiments C.

The experiments are performed by means of stratified 10-fold cross-validation. Figure 3 shows the architecture of Experiment C.

The results shown in Table 7, illustrate that Word Embeddings based on CBOW (with the exception of Precision) generate the best results. However, the difference to skip grams is marginal. This finding is also interesting about the fact that Mikolov et al. reported better results with Skip Grams. Furthermore, the assumption is confirmed that the embeddings created in the context are better than those created outside the context are.

Table 7. Results of the deep learning approach with the used word embeddings.

Embeddings	Accuracy	Precision	Recall	F1
CBOW	86,62%	84,11%	79,29%	81,46%
Skip Gram	86,05%	84,71%	77,77%	80,78%
DM	84,00%	79,54%	77,16%	78,18%
DBOW	83,73%	79,04%	76,77%	77,74%
Reimers	82,05%	79,43%	70,88%	74,14%

The Doc2Vec results should also be highlighted: With 4,658 emails, the training data was considerably lower compared to the two million emails at Word2Vec. Nevertheless, the results are already comparable with the results of approach A. Moreover, Le and Mikolov [32] expect DM to generate better results than DBOW.

4   Summary and Future Work

On the background of optimizing the analysis of the polarity of German-language emails at the document level, three approaches to sentiment analysis were compared in experiments: Approach A combines machine learning methods and sentiment dictionaries. Approach B extends this with additional feature extraction methods. Experiment C combines Word Embeddings and CNN. Measured against the quality criteria of the best results per approach, approach C dominates all cases (see Table 8).

Table 8. Comparison of the best results of the approaches A, B and C.

	Accuracy	Precision	Recall	F1
A	83,82%	82,26%	74,55%	77,78%
B	85,03%	81,22%	77,98%	79,49%
C	86,62%	84,11%	79,29%	81,46%

Approach C classifies polarity best, while approach B generates better results than approach A. It should be noted that this confirmation only applies to the best results. Within the experiments a dependence of the results on the respective method combination is visible. Thus, the results of a machine learning method based on sentiment lexicons are not necessarily better by adding further feature extraction methods. Furthermore, the deep learning approach, depending on the word embedding that is used, is not always better than an alternative from A or B.

However, the insights gained are still remarkably relevant for the customer service of companies. In particular, the Deep Learning approach is suitable for automatically identifying negative sentiment in customer e-mails in order to treat the respective concerns preferentially and to identify negative effects for the company at an early stage and, at best, to avoid them.

For further research, the investigation of the combination of machine learning methods itself offers further potential. A significant improvement of the approaches can be assumed in the inclusion of further linguistic specifics such as the recognition of sarcasm and irony.

References

1. Gupta, N., Gilbert, M., Di Fabbrizio, G.: Emotion detection in email customer care. In: Inkpen, D., Strapparava, C. (eds.) Proceedings of the NAACL HLT 2010 Workshop on Computational Approaches to Analysis and Generation of Emotion in Text, pp. 10–16. Association for Computational Linguistics, Los Angeles (2010)

2. Radicati Group: Email statistics report, 2018–2022 - executive summary, pp. 1–4. https://doi. org/10.18356/1de36bac-en

3. Borele, P., Borikar, D.: An approach to sentiment analysis using artificial neural network with comparative analysis of different techniques. IOSR J. Comput. Eng. **2**(18), 64–69 (2016)

4. Nasukawa, T., Yi, J.: Sentiment analysis: capturing favorability using natural language processing. In: Proceedings of the 2nd International Conference on Knowledge Capture, 23–26 October, 2003, Florida, USA, pp. 70–77. ACM Press, New York (2003). https://doi.org/10. 1145/945645.945658

5. Agarwal, A., Xie, B., Vovsha, I., Rambow, O., Passonneau, R.: Sentiment analysis of twitter data. In: Proceedings of the Workshop on Language in Social Media LSM 2011, Portland 2011, pp. 30–38, Stroudsburg (2011)

6. Bravo-Marquez, F., Mendoza, M., Poblete, B.: Meta-level sentiment models for big social data analysis. Knowl. Based Syst. **69**, 86–99 (2014)

7. Ravi, K., Ravi, V.: A survey on opinion mining and sentiment analysis: tasks, approaches and applications. Knowl. Based Syst. **89**, 14–46 (2015). https://doi.org/10.1016/j.knosys.2015. 06.015

8. Scholz, T., Conrad, S., Hillekamps, L.: Opinion mining on a german corpus of a media response analysis. In: Sojka, P., Horák, A., Kopeček, I., Pala, K. (eds.) TSD 2012. LNCS (LNAI), vol. 7499, pp. 39–46. Springer, Heidelberg (2012). https://doi.org/10.1007/978-3-642-32790-2_4

9. Steinbauer, F., Kröll, M.: Sentiment analysis for German Facebook pages. In: Métais, E., Meziane, F., Saraee, M., Sugumaran, V., Vadera, S. (eds.) NLDB 2016. LNCS, vol. 9612, pp. 427–432. Springer, Cham (2016). https://doi.org/10.1007/978-3-319-41754-7_44

10. Waltinger, U.: GermanPolarityClues: a lexical resource for German sentiment analysis. In: Calzolari, N., Choukri, K., Maegaard, B., Mariani, J., Odijk, J., Piperidis, S., et al. (eds.) Proceedings of the 7th Conference on International Language Resources and Evaluation (LREC-10), pp. 1638–1642. European Language Resources Association, Valletta (2010)

11. Cao, Y., Xu, R., Chen, T.: Combining convolutional neural network and support vector machine for sentiment classification. In: Zhang, X., Sun, M., Wang, Z., Huang, X. (eds.) CNCSMP 2015. CCIS, vol. 568, pp. 144–155. Springer, Singapore (2015). https://doi.org/10.1007/978-981-10-0080-5_13

12. Sebastiani, F.: Machine learning in automated text categorization. ACM Comput. Surv. (CSUR) **34**(1), 1–47 (2002). https://doi.org/10.1145/505282.505283

13. Vinodhini, G., Chandrasekaran, R.M.: Sentiment analysis and opinion mining: a survey. Int. J. Adv. Res. Comput. Sci. Softw. Eng. **2**(6), 282–292 (2012)

14. Ohana, B., Tierney, B.: Sentiment classification of reviews using SentiWordNet. In: 9th IT & T Conference, October 2009, pp. 1–9, Dublin (2009) https://doi.org/10.21427/d77s56

15. Stojanovski, D., Strezoski, G., Madjarov, G., Dimitrovski, I.: Twitter sentiment analysis using deep convolutional neural network. In: Onieva, E., Santos, I., Osaba, E., Quintián, H., Corchado, E. (eds.) HAIS 2015. LNCS (LNAI), vol. 9121, pp. 726–737. Springer, Cham (2015). https://doi.org/10.1007/978-3-319-19644-2_60

16. Webster, J., Watson, R.T.: Analyzing the past to prepare for the future: writing a literature review. MIS Q. **26**(2), 13–23 (2002)

17. Prabowo, R., Thelwall, M.: Sentiment analysis: a combined approach. J. Informetr. **3**, 143–157 (2009). https://doi.org/10.1016/j.joi.2009.01.003

18. Haberzettl, M., Markscheffel, B.: A literature analysis for the identification of machine learning and feature extraction methods for sentiment analysis. In: Proceedings of the 13th International Conference on Digital Information Management (ICDIM 2018), pp. 385–391, Berlin (2018). https://doi.org/10.5220/0008114803850391

19. Bütow, F., Schultze, F., Strauch, L.: Semantic search: sentiment analysis with machine learning algorithms on German news articles (2017). http://www.dai-labor.de/fileadmin/Files/Publik atio-nen/Buchdatei/BuetowEtAl–SentimentAnalysis. Accessed 11 May 2019

20. Thelwall, M., Buckley, K., Paltoglou, G., Cai, D., Kappas, A.: Sentiment strength detection in short informal text. J. Am. Soc. Inf. Sci. Technol. **61**(12), 2544–2558 (2010). https://doi.org/10.1002/asi.21416

21. Remus, R., Quasthoff, U., Heyer, G.: SentiWS - a publicly available German-language resource for sentiment analysis. In: Calzolari, N., Choukri, K., Maegaard, B., Mariani, J., et al. (eds.) International Conference on Language Resources and Evaluation, pp. 1168–1171 (2010)

22. Turney, P.D.: Thumbs up or thumbs down? Semantic orientation applied to unsupervised classification of reviews. In: Isabelle, P. (eds.) Proceedings of the 40th Annual Meeting on Association for Computational Linguistics, Philadelphia 2002, pp. 417–424 (2002)

23. Turney, P.D., Littman, M.L.: Measuring praise and criticism. ACM Trans. Inf. Syst. **21**(4), 315–346 (2003). https://doi.org/10.1145/944012.944013

24. Cleve, J., Lämmel, U.: Data Mining. De Gruyter, Oldenbourg (2014)

25. Davis, J., Goadrich, M.: The relationship between Precision-Recall and ROC curves. In: Cohen, W., Moore, A. (eds.) Proceedings of the 23rd International Conference on Machine Learning, Pittsburgh, PA, pp. 233–240 (2006). https://doi.org/10.1145/1143844.1143874

26. Kohavi, R.: A study of cross-validation and bootstrap for accuracy estimation and model selection. In: Mellish, C.S. (eds.) Proceedings of the 14th International Joint Conference on Artificial Intelligence (IJCAI-1995), Montreal, pp. 1137–1143, Morgan Kaufmann Publishers Inc., San Francisco (1995)

27. Markscheffel, B., Haberzettl, M.: Sentiment analysis of German emails: a comparison of two approaches. In: DATA 2019 - Proceedings of the 8th International Conference on Data Science, Technology and Applications, pp. 385–392, SCITEPRESS – Science and Technology Publications (2019)

28. Pang, B., Lee, L.: Opinion mining and sentiment analysis. FNT Inf. Retr. **2**, 1–135 (2008). https://doi.org/10.1561/1500000011

29. Liu, Y., Liu, Z., Chua, T.S., Sun, M.: Topical word embeddings. In: Proceedings of the 29th AAAI Conference on Artificial Intelligence, pp. 2418–2424. AAAI Press, Palo Alto (2015)

30. Neelakantan, A., Shankar, J., Passos, A., McCallum, A.: Efficient non-parametric estimation of multiple embeddings per word in vector space. In: Proceedings of the 2014 Conference on Empirical Methods in Natural Language Processing (EMNLP), Doha, Qatar, pp. 1059–1069. Association for Computational Linguistics (2014). https://doi.org/10.3115/v1/d14-1113

31. Mikolov, T., Chen, K., Corrado, G., Dean, J.: Efficient estimation of word representations in vector space. CoRR http://arxiv.org/abs/1301.3781 (2013)

32. Le, Q.V., Mikolov, T.: Distributed representations of sentences and documents. In: Xing, E.P., Jebara, T. (eds.) Proceedings of the 31st International Conference on Machine Learning - Volume 32 (ICML 2014), vol. 32, pp. 1188–1196, JMLR.org (2014)

33. Reimers, N., Eckle-Kohler, J., Schnober, C., Kim, J., Gurevych, I.: GermEval-2014: nested named entity recognition with neural networks. In: Proceedings of the KONVENS GermEval Shared Task on Named Entity Recognition, Hildesheim, pp. 117–120 (2014)

Industry 4.0: Sensor Data Analysis Using Machine Learning

Nadeem Iftikhar[1]($^{(\boxtimes)}$), Finn Ebertsen Nordbjerg[1], Thorkil Baattrup-Andersen[2], and Karsten Jeppesen[1]

[1] University College of Northern Denmark, 9200 Aalborg, Denmark
{naif,fen,kaje}@ucn.dk
[2] Dolle A/S, 7741 Frøstrup, Denmark
ta@dolle.com

Abstract. The technological revolution, known as industry 4.0, aims to improve efficiency/productivity and reduce production costs. In the Industry 4.0 based smart manufacturing environment, machine learning techniques are deployed to identify patterns in live data by creating models using historical data. These models will then predict previously undetectable incidents. This paper initially performs a descriptive statistics and visualization, subsequently issues like classification of data with imbalanced class distribution are addressed. Then several binary classification-based machine learning models are built and trained for predicting production line disruptions, although only logistic regression and artificial neural networks are discussed in detail. Finally, it evaluates the effectiveness of the machine learning models as well as the overall utilization of the manufacturing operation in terms of availability, performance and quality.

Keywords: Industry 4.0 · Sensor data · Data analysis · Machine learning · Smart manufacturing · Imbalanced data

1 Introduction

The fourth industrial revolution (Industry 4.0) focuses greatly on automation, interconnected devices and sensors, machine learning, data analysis and visualization. Industry 4.0 aims at enhancing productivity by increasing operational efficiency, development of new products, services and business models [1]. Data analysis uses many techniques ranging from statistics to machine learning. In the manufacturing industry, these techniques can be applied to a number of problems including, but not limited to: identify or predict production line interruptions; identify bottlenecks, and optimize the manufacturing processes in order to minimize downtime and maximize productivity. The framework presented in this paper to structure and execute the data analysis and modeling methods is Cross-industry Standard Process for Data Mining (CRISP–DM) [2]. It enlists business objectives, data insight, data preprocessing, modeling and evaluation.

S. Hammoudi et al. (Eds.): DATA 2019, CCIS 1255, pp. 37–58, 2020.
https://doi.org/10.1007/978-3-030-54595-6_3

This work was achieved in collaboration with Dolle [3]. Dolle is a leader in manufacturing of timber loft ladders and is present in more than 40 countries worldwide. Competing globally require an efficient production process and a rigorous quality control in order to maintain profitability and productivity. This has led the development of these sensor data analysis and machine learning techniques. A main goal of building machine learning methods for Dolle is to reduce downtime and improve profitability by predicting production line disruptions.

This paper is a significant extension of our previous conference paper [4]. In the previous work a data pipeline to handle data acquisition, processing and analysis was proposed. An exploratory analysis of the data was provided. Further, a statistically based machine learning model to predict costly production line disruptions was also presented using a real-life case study. This paper extends [4] by building multiple machine learning models and evaluating the performance of these models to select the best one(s) and it also presents techniques to handle imbalanced data.

To summarize, the main contributions in this paper are as follow:

- Providing an in-depth descriptive statistics and visualization.
- Presenting techniques for handling imbalanced data.
- Building multiple machine learning models for predicting costly production line disruptions.
- Comprehensive evaluation of the equipment effectiveness and the performance of the proposed models.

The paper is structured as follows. Section 2 describes the objectives and requirements from a business perspective. Section 3 gives initial insights about data. Section 4 provides descriptive statistics. Section 5 presents the machine learning models. Section 6 evaluates the equipment effectiveness and performance of the models. Section 7 presents the related work. Section 8 concludes the paper and points out the future research directions.

2   Objectives

The focus of this section is to understand the basic concepts of smart manufacturing in consultation with domain experts. The objectives of the project are derived from the viewpoint and requirements of Dolle. Properly scrutinized they are then translated to data science problems. From a business perspective Dolle's primary questions include: How long does it take, before the right output pace is achieved after a machine is started (see Fig. 1)? Relating to the output pace being defined as the average time between the start of manufacturing of one unit and the start of manufacturing of the next unit: What is the current rate? What is the optimal rate? What are the causes and length of production stops? In addition, Dolle would like to know the amount of time spent changing from one product type to another.

After defining the goals in business terminology, these goals are then translated to technical terms, known as data mining goals. A non-exhaustive list of the data mining goals is presented below:

Fig. 1. Three-section timber loft ladder at Dolle's assembly line.

1. Frequency of machine stops due to faulty strings/screw errors as well as total downtime of the machine due to faulty strings/screw errors?
2. What is the production rate (pace) of the machine?
3. What is the maximum pace?
4. When do delays occur and for how long and are there any discernible patterns?
5. Based on historical patterns, predict machine stops and/or how to prevent them?
6. What is the overall downtime of a machine and/or what are the costs?

In general, production with 80–85 % efficiency is considered very efficient. It will be interesting to investigate every predicted and unpredicted incident during production: What caused it? Can it be predicted(if unpredicted) and mitigated? Some of the known challenges during production are: breakdowns, changeovers, minor stoppage, reduced speed, defects and setup scrap. Hence, the quality of the manufacturing process can be measured by calculating the *Overall Equipment Effectiveness (OEE)* [5]. OEE is the most common standard for measuring manufacturing productivity. It calculates the percentage of manufacturing time that is truly productive.

3   Initial Insights About Data

This section starts with the data acquisition and proceeds with the activities which describe how initial insights of the data are obtained. Firstly, the data acquisition is described and hereafter, activities that provide understanding of the data are discussed. These activities include getting the first insight into the data, identifying data for analysis purposes, discovering data quality issues and/or detecting interesting subsets to form hypothesis regarding previously undetected patterns. The data provided by Dolle is machine data and enterprise resource management (ERP) system data (Fig. 2). Machine data describe the state of sensors and alarms, whereas, ERP data provides information about products, job executions and work calendar. The machine data consists of only binary values (0's and 1's). The number of attributes depends on the specific machine in question. The product data set contains 85 attributes, the job execution data set contains 69 attributes and the work calendar data set has 10

Machine data from sensors & alarm data   Product & schedule data from ERP system

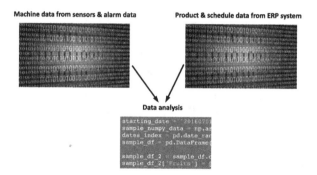

Fig. 2. Data overview.

attributes. Each job represents a specific business task that is carried out for a certain time interval to produce particular type of ladders. The structure of the data does not conform to any standard and additionally no assumptions can be made that two identical units or machines display identical structures.

Dolle's case study clearly illustrate the challenges faced in data analysis in the smart manufacturing industry. The data analysis methods presented in this paper, however, are general. In this case study machine data from the production facility are logged in order to record the states of the machines at any given time. The logged data is initially kept in detailed format in different database tables (a separate table for each machine). As mentioned above, each machine has a different set of sensors/attributes, for that reason only one of the machines is considered for demonstration purposes. The selected machine (*Machine_1*) consists of the following attributes: *(DateTime, MachineOn, PaceIn, PaceOut, FaultyString, ScrewError, Alarm)*. The DateTime identifies a recording of a date and time event at one second granularity. The *MachineOn* sensor indicates the machine is running for a given job. The *PaceIn* or entrance of a beam/string sensor represents an incoming string. The *PaceOut* or exit of a ladder sensor represents an outgoing ladder. The *FaultyString* sensor signifies the quality of the string. Bended or twisted strings are regarded as faulty strings. The *ScrewError* sensor corresponds to the screwing machine that screw strings into place. Finally, the *Alarm* or Error sensor represents a general abnormality in the machine. For example, a string is struck in the machine. An alarm for extended time may result in a machine stoppage.

In order to provide a snapshot of data, a real machine data set provided by Dolle is used. The snapshot contains 7 attributes for job no. 307810 to produce a CF (ClickFix) type ladder. In Table 1, initially the granularity of the detailed data is at *second by job by machine*. Ex: Row number 1 reads as follows: *DateTime*=19-02-2019 09:53:07 (represents: second granularity. It is important to note that if the next row has same values as the previous row in that case the next row will not be logged to the database causing the time discontinuity), *MachineOn*=1 (represents: machine is running), *PaceIn*=0 (represents: no string is entering), *PaceOut*=1 (represents: exiting of the ladder), *FaultyString*=0 (represents: the quality of the string is OK), *ScrewError*=0 (represents: no error in the screwing

Table 1. Sensor and alarm data [4].

Id	DateTime	MachineOn	PaceIn	PaceOut	FaultyString	ScrewError	Alarm
.	.	.	.	.	.	.	.
1	19-02-2019 09:53:07	1	0	1	0	0	0
2	19-02-2019 09:53:09	1	1	1	0	0	0
3	19-02-2019 09:53:10	1	0	1	0	0	0
4	19-02-2019 09:53:12	1	0	0	0	0	0
.	.	.	.	.	.	.	.
5	19-02-2019 09:53:56	1	1	0	0	0	0
6	19-02-2019 09:53:58	1	0	0	0	0	0
7	19-02-2019 09:54:04	1	0	1	0	0	0
8	19-02-2019 09:54:09	1	0	0	0	0	0
9	19-02-2019 09:54:14	1	1	0	0	0	0
10	19-02-2019 09:54:15	1	0	0	0	0	0
11	19-02-2019 09:54:20	1	0	0	0	0	1
12	19-02-2019 09:54:21	1	1	0	0	0	1
.	.	.	.	.	.	.	.
13	19-02-2019 09:56:14	1	0	0	0	1	0
14	19-02-2019 09:56:16	1	0	0	0	0	0
15	19-02-2019 09:56:29	1	0	1	0	0	0
16	19-02-2019 09:56:31	1	1	1	0	0	0
17	19-02-2019 09:56:33	1	0	0	0	0	0
.	.	.	.	.	.	.	.

Table 2. ERP system data.

JobId	ProductId	JobStart	JobEnd	JobFinished	GoodQuality
307810	524167	19-02-2019 09:34:23	19-02-2019 10:17:43	0	0
370810	524167	19-02-2019 10:28:28	19-02-2019 11:23:04	1	70

machine) and *Alarm*=0 (represents: no abnormality in the machine). Whereas, Id is an abstract attribute and used only for row identification purposes. Similarly, row number 13 reads as follows: *DateTime*=19-02-2019 09:56:14, *MachineOn*=1, *PaceIn*=0, *PaceOut*=0 (represents: no ladder is exiting), *FaultyString*=0, *ScrewError*=1 (represents: an error in the screwing machine) and *Alarm*=0 (represents: no abnormality in the machine identified yet). Further, initial look into the data in Table 1 reveals some interesting facts, such as, the ladder is produced (row 7) in 09:54:04 − 09:53:07 = 57 s (average pace), where as, the next ladder is produced (row 15) in 09:56:29 − 09:54:04 = 145 s. The delay in the production of the next ladder is due to the fact that an alarm has been triggered (row 11) and a screwing machine error has also caused the delay (row 13).

Further, Table 2 displays some of the attributes of the ERP system data that may be used for analysis purposes *(JobId, ProductId, JobStart (date and time), JobEnd (date and time), JobFinished, GoodQuality)*. As mentioned earlier, ERP system data has 164 attributes, in total. The *JobId* represents the given job. The *productId* represents a specific product. The *JobStart* represents the date and time when a job starts. Similarly, *JobEnd* represents the date and time when a job ends. A job may be carried out in multiple time intervals as seen in Table 2. The

JobFinished characterizes if the current job has finished and the *GoodQuality* attribute represents the number of acceptable quality products produced.

Furthermore, several interesting subsets may be identified from the initial insights of the data sets that leads to hypothesis regarding initial data patterns. For example, whether screwing machine errors causes more machine stops than faulty strings.

4   Data Preprocessing

This section provides insight into the business problems before performing data modeling. The data preprocessing phase include activities, such as data selection, data transformation, data cleaning and data validation. These tasks may be performed several times and not in any given order. During this phase important issues like selecting the relevant data, cleaning of data and discarding unacceptable data are addressed. Additionally, it is determined how the ERP system data can be integrated into the final data sets. Some of the cleaning techniques discussed in [6] may be applicable here as well. Metadata originating from discussions between data scientists and domain experts has been crucial to the process of data validation. Some meta issues cannot be inferred from the sensor data but require domain expertise like: "is the machine output reliable, when the 'error sensor or alarm' is 'on', can this be verified?". Contrary to logic, the answer is "yes", as during production of certain types of ladders the alarm is disregarded. Another anomaly is that the logged data showed twice the numbers of ladders produced than actually was produced. The reason for this is that the pace out sensor was triggered twice in the process of folding the ladder, this was subsequently corrected in the logging process.

The other aspect of data validity is "adequacy", "is there sufficient amount of data available to make valid predictions?". By examining data from one of the ladder machines producing no apparent output the question "why", arises. In this case, the machine in question was jammed and the ladder machine could not deliver its output and hence stood still. An additional sensor would have enabled the predictive ability to identify why no output was produced. Further, decisions about the format of the final data sets and time granularity are also made at this phase. When addressing the data granularity, the maximum data sample rate is "1 s", however, the data set shows that more than one sensor status changed within the limited time (see row 16 and 17 in Table 1). At 09:56:31 row 16 shows that the pace in and pace out sensors both have values "1". At 09:56:32 no sensor changed state hence no registration was recorded. At 09:56:33 row 17 shows that the pace in and pace out sensors both have values "0", which means that multiple sensors changed state within the granularity of 1 s. Based on this observation, and as it is important to know if *PaceIn* follows *PaceOut* or *PaceOut* follows *PaceIn* in order to form a relation the used method of checking/recording sensors status at a granularity of 1 s is not sufficient. A finer granularity, such as 500 ms or even finer is required.

Another aspect of the data preprocessing phase is to perform descriptive statistical analysis and visualization. The focus of this paper is on statistical analysis rather than data cleansing. Hence, only descriptive analysis and visualization are further discussed.

4.1 Descriptive Statistics and Visualization

Descriptive data analysis is primarily a graphic approach that provides a first insight into the data. The two main characteristics of descriptive analysis are *honesty* and *trust*. Honesty means that the data scientist should be open to all possibilities prior to exploring the data, whereas, trust means that the impression, data is making, is not deceiving. There are no formal/standard set of rules that can be used in descriptive analysis, however, common approaches are: summary statistics, correlation, visualization and aggregation. Summary statistics or univariate analysis is the first step that helps us to understand data. Univariate analysis is the simplest form of data analysis where the data being analyzed contains only one variable. Further, data correlation or multivariate analysis helps us to find relationships between two or more variables. Finding connections between variables also has a crucial impact on choosing and building the predictive model(s).

Table 3. Univariate analysis.

	MachineOn	PaceIn	PaceOut	FaultyString	ScrewError	Alarm
Mean	0.98	0.36	0.12	0.03	0.08	0.51
Std. Deviation	0.15	0.48	0.16	0.15	0.27	0.49
Minimum	0	0	0	0	0	0
Maximum	1	1	1	1	1	1
Skewness	−6.59	0.62	1.21	6.18	3.08	−0.49
Kurtosis	41.50	−1.61	−0.53	36.24	7.53	−1.99

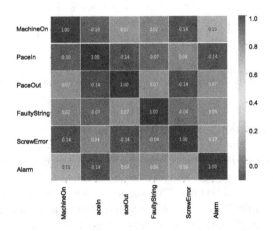

Fig. 3. Sensor and alarm correlation heat map.

Data visualization helps us to gain perspective into the data, such as to find anomalies or to detect outliers. Finally, data aggregation helps us to group data from coarser to finer granularities in order to improve understanding due to the limited nature of data. Table 3 (univariate descriptive analysis) shows mean, standard deviation, minimum, maximum, skewness and kurtosis. The most interesting findings in Table 3 are skewness and kurtosis. Skewness is a measure of symmetry and kurtosis is a measure of tailedness. Table 3, illustrates that *MachineOn* variable is extremely skewed towards right side (98% of the rows shows that machine is on). *FaultyString* and *ScrewError* variables are also extremely skewed towards left. Similarly, *MachineOn* and *FaultyString* variables have very high positive Kurtosis values that means that *MachineOn* is substantially peaked towards 1 and *FaultyString* is peaked towards 0. As, for perfectly symmetrical data the skewness is 0 and kurtosis is 3 for that reason it can be concluded that at least half of the variables of the machine data are highly skewed/peaked towards either 1 or 0.

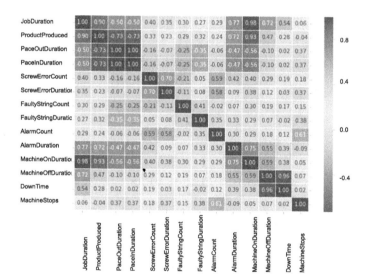

Fig. 4. Sensor and alarm (aggregated at daily granularity) correlation heat map [4].

In addition, correlation matrices are constructed to carry out a multivariate descriptive analysis. The correlation matrix of the sensor and the alarm variables at 1 s granularity (Fig. 3) shows no interdependence. For that reason, data is being aggregated at daily granularity by job. Figure 4, shows some interesting positive and negative correlations. The correlations with respect to *PaceIn, PaceOut, ScrewError, FaultyString, MachineOff*, number of unplanned *MachineStops* and *DownTime* are of particular interest. Due to the fact that one of the main aims of this analysis is to figure out which factors negatively impact the production and/or triggers machine stoppage. The correlation coefficient value

locates between -1 and $+1$. The coefficient values between *PaceIn/PaceOut*
and *FaultyString/MachineStops* (-0.35 and $+0.37$) indicate both weak negative and positive correlations. Further, the coefficient values between *ScrewEr-
ror/FaultyString* and *MachineStops* ($+0.37$ and $+0.38$) indicate weak positive
correlations. Moreover, the coefficient values between *DownTime* and *JobDura-
tion/MachineOff* duration ($+0.54$ and $+0.96$) indicate moderate to strong positive correlations. Hence, it can be concluded that *ScrewError* and *FaultyString*
both have weak to moderate effect on the number of unplanned *MachineStops*,
however, the duration of these stops have a strong positive correlation with
machine *DownTime*.

The status of the machine, screw errors and faulty strings can also be viewed
in Fig. 5 (a-c). It is quite obvious that screwing machine errors and faulty strings
are causing a high percentage of machine stoppages (white holes in the data set).

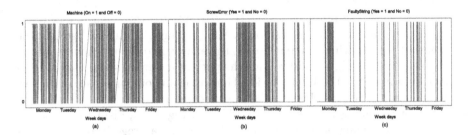

Fig. 5. Machine, faulty string and screw error status.

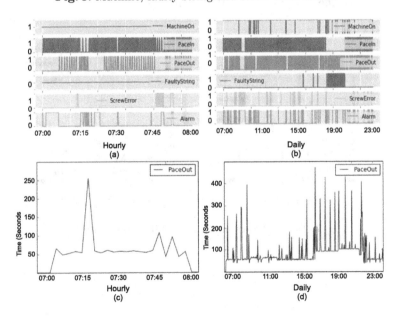

Fig. 6. Sensor and alarm data overview [4].

Further, Fig. 6 (a-d) provide an overview of the sensor and alarm data at hourly and daily granularities, respectively. It is seen in Fig. 6 (a) that the machine is on almost all the time. The pace of the incoming strings is also fine showing very few stops, however, the pace of outgoing ladders show some stops. The outgoing pace slows down (Fig. 6 (c)) between 07:15 and 07:20 as well as between 07:45 and 07:55. These slow downs are partly caused by errors in the screwing machine, and additionally these slow downs trigger the alarm. Similarly, Fig. 6 (b) demonstrates that the machine is on most of the time, incoming pace slows down between 16:00 and 21:00 mainly due to faulty strings that also slow down the outgoing pace (Fig. 6 (d)).

Moreover, the results of the detailed analysis at daily granularity are illustrated in Fig. 7 (a-b). Figure 7 (a), shows that there are opportunities both for undertaking more jobs as well as for improving the machine on duration. Likewise, machine off duration and downtime are also quite significant. Screwing machine errors are little more frequent than faulty strings and noticeably the alarm duration is also quite high. Figure 7 (b) presents the frequency of products produced, screwing machines errors, faulty strings, alarms and stops. The frequency of the screwing machine errors, the alarms and the machine stops are noticeable. Further, Fig. 8 (a-b) reveals the pace of incoming strings and outgoing ladders. Figure 8 (a), exhibits the ideal incoming and outgoing pace of the two main categories of ladders. The ideal average incoming pace is 9.5 s, whereas, the ideal average outgoing pace is 60 s. In addition, Fig. 8 (b), displays the actual incoming and outgoing pace at daily level. The actual average incoming pace is 15.5 s and the actual outgoing pace is 93.5 s. Hence, there is a clear possibility of optimizing both the incoming and outgoing pace.

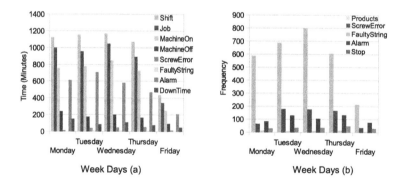

Fig. 7. Detailed data analysis at daily granularity [4].

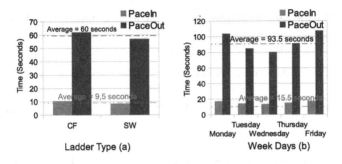

Fig. 8. In and out pace.

To summarize, the descriptive analysis discloses that data is not uniformly distributed and almost half of the variables are highly skewed. Moreover, due to the binary nature of data, correlation matrices only reveal weak interdependence between the variables. In addition, visualisation and aggregations confirm that screwing machines errors are causing more machine stops than faulty strings and that machine downtime needs to be reduced. In addition, to give these findings a commercial value a learning loop must be introduced where the finding are followed by actions and new data is compared to "old" data to check if actions have the anticipated effect.

5   Predictive Analysis

This section introduces the basic concepts of machine learning based models, data aggregation and explains some of the key issues such as imbalanced data. One of the main goals of this case study is "to predict the machine's unplanned stops depending on historical consequences/patterns". Based on the kind of data available and the research question/goal, supervised machine learning is used to predict when the machine is going to stop. Supervised learning algorithms train from historical data, such as machine is on "1" or off "0". The algorithm determines which label should be given to new data based on historical patterns. Most commonly used classification algorithms in machine learning are logistic regression, artificial neural networks, support vector machines (SVM), k-nearest neighbors (KNN), decision trees, auto-regressive integrated moving average (ARIMA), naive bayes and others [7]. In this paper, logistic regression, support vector machines, k-nearest neighbors, decision trees and artificial neural networks are used, however, only logistic regression and neural networks are further explained.

5.1   Machine Learning Based Models

Logistic Regression. Logistic regression is one of the frequently used algorithm for binary classification. It predicts the binary (0 or 1) outcome by computing its probability.

The following set of equations present the logistic model for binary data:

$$y = \beta_0 + \beta_1 X_1 + \beta_2 X_2 + ... + \beta_n X_n \qquad (1)$$

Equation 1, is a linear regression equation, where y is dependent variable and X_1, X_2 ... and X_n are explanatory variables. β_0 is the intercept and β_1, β_2 ... and β_n represent the slope of the regression line.

$$p = 1/(1 + e^{-y}) \qquad (2)$$

The logistic function presented in Eq. 2 is the sigmoid function. The sigmoid function is a mathematical function having an "S" shaped curve (sigmoid curve). The logistic function restricts the probability (p) value between zero and one.

$$p = 1/(1 + e^{-(\beta_0 + \beta_1 X_1 + \beta_2 X_2 + ... + \beta_n X_n)}) \qquad (3)$$

Finally, Eq. 3 is applying Sigmoid function on the linear regression.

Artificial Neural Networks. Artificial neural networks or neural networks consist of algorithms that work in the same way as nerve cells or neurons in human brain. Neural networks are commonly used to recognize patterns and suites well for binary classification. Similar to logistic regression, artificial neural network classification model also uses activation function to generate a probability in the range of 0 to 1 in order to predict the outcome.

The following set of equations present artificial neural network model for binary data:

$$z_j = \sum_{i=1}^{n} (w_{1,i} x_i + b_i), 1 \leq j \leq m \qquad (4)$$

Equation 4, is a summation equation, where m represents the number of neurons in the hidden layer, n indicates the number of inputs, x_i represents the sensor values, $w_{1,i}$ represents the first set of weights and b_i is the bias value that intends to adjust the output.

$$h_j = f(z_j) = max(0, z_j), 1 \leq j \leq m \qquad (5)$$

The hidden layer activation function presented in Eq. 5 is the ReLU function, where z_j is the input to a neuron and m is the number of neurons in the hidden layer. The ReLU function is a mathematical function that stands for rectified linear unit. The activation function applies a ReLU function in order to restrict the z_j value between zero and infinity. The ReLU is half rectified (from bottom), which means that $f(z_j)$ is zero when z_j is less than zero and $f(z_j)$ is equal to z_j when z_j is above or equal to zero.

$$y = \sum_{i=1}^{m} w_{2,i} h_i \qquad (6)$$

Equation 6, is a summation equation, where m indicates the number of neurons in the hidden layer, h_i represents the intermediate results of the neurons in the hidden layer and $w_{2,i}$ represents the second set of weights.

$$f(y) = 1/(1 + e^{-y}) \tag{7}$$

The output layer activation function presented in Eq. 7 is the sigmoid function in order to restrict the final output value between zero and one.

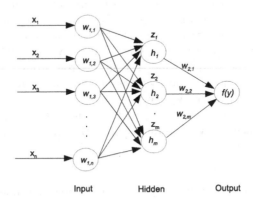

Fig. 9. Single hidden layer artificial neural network.

Further, a single hidden layer neural network for the sensor binary data is presented in Fig. 9. Where, the input layer consists of the sensor values, such as pace in, pace out and so on. The hidden (middle) layer, uses Rectified Linear Unit (ReLU) activation function. The purpose of ReLU is to calculate the intermediate result values for each node in the hidden layer (Eq. 5). The input to the ReLU activation function is the sum of the products of the input sensor values with the first set of weights and the output is the intermediate result values. Finally, the output layer, uses Sigmoid activation function to determine the final output value. The input to the Sigmoid activation function is the sum of the products of the hidden layer intermediate result values with the second set of weights and the output is the final output value. Initially, the sets of weights are selected randomly by using Gaussian distribution (forward propagation) and afterwards backward propagation computes the margin of error of the final output value and update the sets of weights.

5.2 Data Aggregation

In order to compare the performance of the proposed machine models it is possible to make changes in the structure of the data. One of the options is to use aggregates for the reason that there may be some patterns in the sensor data that may not be identified at a row level.

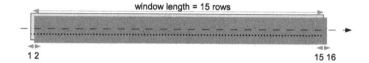

Fig. 10. Rolling window.

A rolling/sliding window technique is used in this paper to calculate an aggregated outcome on a fixed sized window (15 consecutive sensor readings/rows) and using it for prediction. In rolling window, the window size remains fixed and it moves forward one reading (row) at the time and recalculate the outcome. Figure 10 demonstrates the rolling window, where first window contains row from 1 to 15, the second window contains row from 2 to 16 and so on. The aggregated outcome may be useful in the circumstances where a group of sensor data readings/rows may provide better prediction, than a single data reading/row. To question that whether detailed data or aggregated data achieve better prediction accuracy will be further investigated in Sect. 6.

5.3 Imbalanced Data

In this subsection, four classification based supervised machine learning models are used to predict that whether the machine is on or off. Table 4, demonstrates the *accuracy* of these models. Accuracy is a commonly used approach in classification models. It checks the percentage of correct predictions [8]. The accuracy of the models with detailed data is 98% and with aggregated data, it is 90%, which means that the models are only predicting the majority class that is "machine is on". As demonstrated in the descriptive analysis (Sect. 4) the data set is not uniformly distributed.

Table 4. Predicted accuracy of the models on imbalanced data.

	Detailed data	Aggregated data
Logistic regression	98%	90%
k-nearest neighbors	98%	90%
Support vector machine	98%	91%
Decision tree	98%	91%

Similarly, Fig. 11, confirms that Machine on/off data is completely imbalanced. Out of 1.2 million instances only in 25,000 instances the machine is off. Even though the duration of these stops (downtime) is considerable (Fig. 7 (a)), their frequency is still only 2%. Meanwhile, the majority of the machine learning algorithms presume that the data samples are divided equally among the classes, causing the predictions for minority target class "machine is off" to leads to incorrect results.

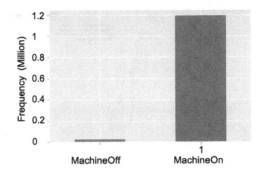

Fig. 11. Machine On/Off histogram.

5.4   Random Data Sampling

As the minority target class "machine is off" is the main focus of prediction the data set has to be resampled. Two common approaches are *oversampling* which is adding instances of the minority class "machine is off" and *undersampling* which is deleting instances of the majority class "machine is on" [9]. In this paper, both undersampling and oversampling are used to adjust the class distribution. Undersampling divides the machine on/off frequency into a 50/50 ratio that means, randomly selecting 25,000 instances where "machine is on" and 25,000 instances where "machine is off". Undersampling, dramatically reduces the sample size by discarding useful data, however, the predictions are not biased. Conversely, oversampling creates synthetic data from the minority class to reach an equal balance between the minority and majority classes. In oversampling, most of the data is retained since no rows are deleted. Oversampling increases the chances of *overfitting* as it duplicates existing data. Overfitting occurs when a model can memorize the training data. Based on the memorization it makes correct predictions only if the test data is exactly the same as the training data. With all other datasets the predictions will be incorrect.

Moreover, in order to decide which machine learning model(s) will be more effective in correctly identifying the status of the machine (on or off) in the random undersampling subset, *receiver operating characteristic curve (ROC)* [8] is used. ROC curve is a graph showing the performance of a binary classification model indicating how accurately the model separate between two events e.g. if a machine is on or off. Figure 12 demonstrate that in detailed and aggregated data in the random undersampling subset, logistic regression and support vector machine models achieve quite a good performance in distinguishing between the positive and the negative values. The ROC curve scores of these two models are 0.88 and 0.75, respectively. Later in this paper (Sect. 6), a neural network is created and its accuracy is compared with one of the best models, logistic regression or support vector machine using as well undersampled as oversampled data.

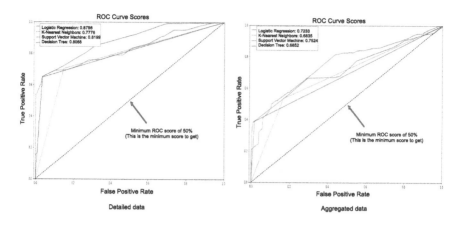

Fig. 12. ROC curves (undersampling).

6   Evaluation

6.1   Overall Equipment Effectiveness

In this section Dolle's manufacturing process is evaluated. This is done by computing the Overall Equipment Effectiveness (OEE) of the manufacturing process. OEE calculates the percentage of manufacturing time that is actually productive. It can be used as a benchmark as well as a baseline. It is one of the most widely used standards to calculate productivity in manufacturing industry. In general, OEE consists of three factors, which are *availability*, *performance* and *quality* [5]. Availability considers all the incidents that stop the planned production. Performance considers those events that causes the manufacturing process to run at less optimal speed. Where as, quality takes into consideration the part of the manufactured products that do not meet quality standards. An OEE score of 100% means that the manufacturing is going along at a perfect pace, without any unplanned stops and producing only good quality products.

Table 5. Dolle's data for the morning shift.

Item	Data
Shift length	510 min
Breaks	60 min
Downtime (planned/unplanned stops)	80 min
Ideal time to produce a single ladder	60 s
Total count	260 ladders
Reject count	2 ladders

Based on the items and data mentioned in Table 5 the OEE can be computed. The OEE will provide a clear picture of the productivity and possibilities for improvements. In order to calculate OEE, the following steps are performed. First, *Planned Production Time (PPT)* and *Run Time (RT)* are calculated. The Planned Production Time is the standard shift time excluding the planned breaks, such as lunch/coffee breaks as well as shift change over time. The Run Time is the actual time of production excluding both the planned and unplanned stops, such as job/product switch over stops, stops caused by faulty strings or by screwing machine error and so on. Afterwards, *Good Count (GC)* is calculated by rejecting the defected ladders.

PPT: Shift Length - Breaks = 510 min − 60 min = 450 min

RT: PPT - Stop Time = 450 min − 80 min = 370 min

GC: Total Count - Reject Count = 260 ladders − 2 ladder = 258 ladders

Next, *Availability (A)*, *Performance (P)* and *Quality (Q)* are to be calculated. Availability is the time when the manufacturing process is not running or the machine is "OFF" for some reasons. Availability takes machine failure (unplanned stops) and setup for next job and/or adjustments (planned stops) into account. Performance, estimates that whether the process is running at its optimal pace and quality concerns with quality standards of the products being produced.

A: RT/PPT = 370 min/450 min = 0.8222 = 82.22%

P: (Ideal Production Time * Total Count)/RT =
(60 s * 260 ladders)/(370 * 60 s) = 0.7027 = 70.27%

Q: Good Count/Total count = 258 ladders/260 ladders = 0.9923 = 99.23%

Finally, the OEE score is computed by multiplying the availability, performance and quality.

OEE: A * P * Q = 0.8222 * 0.7027 * 0.9923 = 0.5733 = 57.33%

An OEE score of 57.33% is fairly typical for automate manufacturing industry, however, it indicates there is significant opportunity for improvement in performance. The performance score can be improved by reducing the switch over time between the jobs, by identifying the reasons for machine stops and finally by tackling the major cause(s) of downtime and so on. An OEE score around 85% is considered a world class for automate manufacturing, where as, an OEE score of 40% or below is considered low.

Table 6. OEE data for four sequential weeks.

	Week 1	Week 2	Week 3	Week 4	Average
OEE	59%	56%	63%	66%	61%
Availability	90%	89%	91%	90%	90%
Performance	66%	63%	71%	75%	68.75%
Quality	99%	98%	97%	99%	98.50%

For better understanding, OEE data for four sequential weeks is computed. Table 6, shows an average OEE number (61%) that captures, how well Dolle is doing and the three numbers that summarize the primary types of losses (Availability, Performance, and Quality). To conclude, an average OEE score of 61% is fairly typical for automate manufacturers, however, it shows that there is considerable scope for improvement, specially the performance loss factor draws attention.

6.2 Testing of Machine Learning Models

In this section, a single hidden layer neural network is compared against the logistic regression model using both undersample and oversample data set in order to see which of these two models has a better accuracy of detecting machine on/off cases. In Sect. 5, both logistic regression and support vector machine models performed well, however, logistic regression is preferred to compare against neural network. The reason is that logistic regression is also considered as a single layer neural network and particularly in this paper both of them are using logistic sigmoid function. In this testing phase, the models are trained in both the random undersampled and oversampled data set to predict the final results using the original test data.

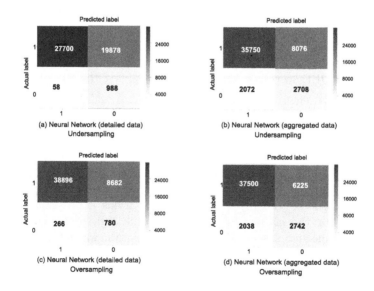

Fig. 13. Confusion matrices.

In order to describe the performance of the classification models, confusion matrix and accuracy are commonly used [8]. A confusion matrix is a table that is used to demonstrate the performance of a classification model based on test data for which both the true positive and true negative values are known, whereas, accuracy means that how often is the classification model is correct. The confusion matrices presented in Fig. 13 can be read as follow:

- Upper Left Square - True Positive (TP): The number of correctly classified "machine on" cases.
- Upper Right Square - False Positive (FP): The number of incorrectly classified cases as "machine is off", whereas the actual label is "machine is on".
- Lower Left Square - False Negative (FN): The number of incorrectly classified cases as "machine is on", whereas the actual label is "machine is off".
- Lower Right Square - True Negative (TN): The number of correctly classified "machine off" cases.

Table 7. Neural network confusion matrices.

	MachineON (TPs)	MachineOFF (TNs)
Detailed data (undersampling)	58%	94%
Aggregated data (undersampling)	82%	57%
Detailed data (oversampling)	81%	75%
Aggregated data (oversampling)	85%	58%

Figure 13, presents confusion matrices for artificial neural network. In Fig. 13(a), the matrix shows that in detailed data using random undersampling subset, out of 47,578 actual instances (first row) of "MachineOn = 1" (true positive), the classifier predicted correctly 27,700 (58%) of them. Whereas, out of 1,046 instances (second row) of "MachineOn=0" (true negative), the classifier predicted correctly 988 (94%) of them. Similarly, Fig. 13(b) presents aggregated data using undersampling subset. The matrix shows that out of 43,826 actual instances of "MachineOn = 1", the classifier predicted correctly 35,750 (82%) of them. Similarly, out of 4,780 instances of "MachineOn=0", the classifier predicted correctly 2,708 (57%) of them. In addition, Fig. 13(c) shows detailed data using oversampling. The matrix shows that when "MachineOn = 1", the classifier predicted correctly 38,896 (81%) and when "MachineOn=0", the classifier predicted correctly 780 (75%). Finally, Fig. 13(d) demonstrates aggregated data using oversampling. The matrix shows that when "MachineOn = 1", the classifier predicted correctly 37,500 (85%) and when "MachineOn=0", the classifier predicted correctly 2,742 (58%). The results are also summarized in Table 7. In conclusion, neural network performed better on both detailed and aggregated test data using undersampling and oversampling to predict machine on/off cases.

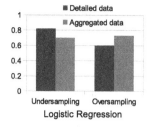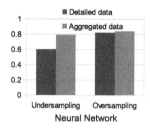

Fig. 14. Classification accuracy.

Furthermore, Fig. 14 shows the accuracy of logistic regression and artificial neural network. It can be seen that the accuracy of logistic regression in detailed data using random undersampling subset is better than neural network, whereas, in aggregated data the neural network performs better. On the other hand, in detailed and aggregated data using random oversampling data set neural network outperforms logistic regression.

7   Related Work

In general, smart manufacturing covers a number of different technologies, such as, data processing or data analytics, connected devices as well as services, robotics and so on.

This section mainly concentrates on the previous work done in relation to predictive data analytics for smart manufacturing. According to Lee et al. [10], smart manufacturing still lacks smart analytical techniques and tools. In order to improve productivity, performance of the manufacturing machinery should be measured and optimized with the help of data analytics technologies. A state-of-the-art review of deep learning techniques for machinery fault diagnosis and predictive analytics is presented by [11]. Similarly, big data analytics in semi-conductor manufacturing industry was studied by [12]. Further, Müller et al. [13], described that big data analytical assets are associated with an average of 3–7% improvement in company productivity. Tao et al. [14], mentioned that data analytics provides an opportunity in the manufacturing industry to adopt data-driven strategies in order to become more competitive. Further, a survey by Kamble et al. [15], highlighted that the manufacturing industry has realized that the data analytics capabilities are must for future growth. Moreover, Auschitzky et al. [16], proposed the use of advanced analytics such as, data visualization, correlation analysis and artificial neural networks to take a deep dive into historical data, in order to identify initial patterns. Predicting the bottlenecks in a production system based on the active periods of the machines using auto-regressive integrated moving average (ARIMA) method was proposed by [17]. Similarly, a big data analytical architecture for product life cycle management as well as cleaner manufacturing was presented by [18]. Furthermore, Shin et al. [19], presented an analytic model for predicting energy consumption of manufacturing machinery. Chen et al. [20], proposed a Quality of Service (QoS) to manage data traffic using deep learning in the small and medium sized industry. Moreover, Candanedo et al. [21], applied machine learning models such as, logistic regression and random forest to predict equipment performance using historical data set. These works focus on various aspects and recent advancements of data analytics technologies/techniques in smart manufacturing. The work presented in this paper is build on top of the ideas presented in those works. Most of them focus on theoretical rather than practical issues in relation to storage, management, processing and prediction of machine-related data, while the focus of this paper is to provide a practical application of the selected data analysis and machine learning techniques.

As, it can be seen from the above mentioned literature, sensor data analysis in manufacturing industry remains briefly addressed, for that reason this paper is among the very few featuring an in-depth sensor data analysis of imbalanced data using machine learning in order to enhance operational efficiency for small and medium sized enterprises (SME) in the manufacturing industry based on the real world case study.

8 Conclusions and Future Work

This paper described the data (descriptive statistics analysis) and machine learning techniques built around the concept of industry 4.0. Descriptive statistics helped to describe and understand the features of data such as, correlation, skewness, kurtosis, class distribution and related. This paper also revealed that descriptive analysis is necessary to build effective machine learning models. Further, various machine learning algorithms such as, logistic regression, neural networks, support vector machines, decision trees and k-nearest neighbors were applied on a historical data set to predict costly production line disruptions. The accuracy of the proposed machine learning models were tested on a real-world data set. The results have validated the effectiveness of the proposed models.

For the future work, a near real-time anomaly detection mechanism using the machine learning models presented in this paper will be developed that can detect events that fail to match an expected pattern. In addition, a near real-time dashboard will be developed to display the input pace, output pace, screw errors, faulty strings, OEE score and more.

Acknowledgement. This research is supported by University College of Northern Denmark - Research and Development funding and Dolle A/S.

References

1. Luz Martín-Peña, M., Díaz-Garrido, E., Sánchez-López, J.M.: The digitalization and servitization of manufacturing: a review on digital business models. Strategic Change **27**(2), 91–99 (2018)
2. Chapman, P., et al.: CRISP-DM 1.0: Step-by-step Data Mining Guide. Technical Report. The CRISP-DM Consortium (2000)

3. Dolle, http://www.dolle.eu. Accessed 11 Nov 2019
4. Iftikhar, N., Andersen, T.B., Nordbjerg, F.E., Bobolea, E., Radu, P.B.: Data analytics for smart manufacturing: a case study. In: 8th International Conference on Data Science, Technology and Applications, pp. 392–399. Scitepress (2019)
5. Overall Equipment Effectiveness (OEE), https://www.oee.com. Accessed 13 Feb 2019
6. Iftikhar, N., Liu, X., Nordbjerg, F.E.: Relational-based sensor data cleansing. In: Morzy, T., Valduriez, P., Bellatreche, L. (eds.) ADBIS 2015. CCIS, vol. 539, pp. 108–118. Springer, Cham (2015). https://doi.org/10.1007/978-3-319-23201-0_13
7. De Gooijer, J.G., Hyndman, R.J.: 25 years of time series forecasting. Int. J. Forecast. **22**(3), 443–473 (2006)
8. Deitel, P.J., Dietal, H.: Intro to python for computer science and data science: learning to program with AI. Big Data and the Cloud. Pearson Education, Incorporated (2020)
9. Gonzàlez, S., García, S., Li, S.T., Herrera, F.: Chain based sampling for monotonic imbalanced classification. Inf. Sci. **474**, 187–204 (2019)
10. Lee, J., Kao, H.-A., Yang, S.: Service innovation and smart analytics for industry 4.0 and big data environment. Procedia CIRP **16**, 3–8 (2014)
11. Wang, J., Ma, Y., Zhang, L., Gao, R.X., Wu, D.: Deep learning for smart manufacturing: methods and applications. J. Manuf. Syst. **48**, 144–156 (2018)
12. Moyne, J., Iskandar, J.: Big data analytics for smart manufacturing: case studies in semiconductor manufacturing. Processes **5**(3), 39–58 (2017)
13. Müller, O., Fay, M., vom Brocke, J.: The effect of big data and analytics on firm performance: an econometric analysis considering industry characteristics. J. Manage. Inf. Syst. **35**(2), 488–550 (2018)
14. Tao, F., Qi, Q., Liu, A., Kusiak, A.: Data-driven smart manufacturing. J. Manuf. Syst. **48**, 157–169 (2018)
15. Kamble, S.S., Gunasekaran, A., Gawankar, S.A.: Sustainable industry 4.0 framework: a systematic literature review identifying the current trends and future perspectives. Process Saf. Environ. Protect. **117**, 408–425 (2018)
16. Auschitzky, E., Markus, H., Agesan, R.: How Big Data can Improve Manufacturing, vol. 822. McKinsey & Company, New York (2014)
17. Subramaniyan, M., Skoogh, A., Salomonsson, H., Bangalore, P., Bokrantz, J.: A data-driven algorithm to predict throughput bottlenecks in a production system based on active periods of the machines. Comput. Ind. Eng. **125**, 533–544 (2018)
18. Zhang, Y., Ren, S., Liu, Y., Si, S.: A big data analytics architecture for cleaner manufacturing and maintenance processes of complex products. J. Cleaner Prod. **142**, 626–641 (2017)
19. Shin, S.J., Woo, J., Rachuri, S.: Predictive analytics model for power consumption in manufacturing. Procedia CIRP **15**, 153–158 (2014)
20. Chen, Z., Luo, L., Yang, H., Yu, J., Wen, M., Zhang, C.: GENIE: QoS-guided dynamic scheduling for CNN-based tasks on SME clusters. In: Design, Automation and Test in Europe Conference and Exhibition, pp. 1599–1602. IEEE (2019)
21. Candanedo, I.S., Nieves, E.H., González, S.R., Martín, M.T.S., Briones, A.G.: Machine learning predictive model for industry 4.0. In: Uden, L., Hadzima, B., Ting, I.-H. (eds.) KMO 2018. CCIS, vol. 877, pp. 501–510. Springer, Cham (2018). https://doi.org/10.1007/978-3-319-95204-8_42

Scalable Architecture, Storage and Visualization Approaches for Time Series Analysis Systems

Eduardo Duarte[1]([✉]), Diogo Gomes[1,2], David Campos[3], and Rui L. Aguiar[1,2]

[1] Department of Electronics, Telecommunications and Informatics, University of Aveiro, Aveiro, Portugal
{emod,dgomes,ruilaa}@ua.pt
[2] Institute of Telecommunications, University of Aveiro, Aveiro, Portugal
[3] Bosch Thermotechnology, Aveiro, Portugal
david.campos@pt.bosch.com

Abstract. In order to adapt to the recent phenomenon of exponential growth of time series data sets in both academic and commercial environments, and with the goal of deriving valuable knowledge from this data, a multitude of analysis software tools have been developed to allow groups of collaborating researchers to find and annotate meaningful behavioral patterns. However, these tools commonly lack appropriate mechanisms to handle massive time series data sets of high cardinality, as well as suitable visual encodings for annotated data. In this paper we conduct a comparative study of architectural, persistence and visualization methods that can enable these analysis tools to scale with a continuously-growing data set and handle intense workloads of concurrent traffic. We implement these approaches within a web platform, integrated with authentication, versioning, and locking mechanisms that prevent overlapping contributions or unsanctioned changes. Additionally, we measure the performance of a set of databases when writing and reading varying amounts of series data points, as well as the performance of different architectural models at scale.

Keywords: Time series · Annotations · Annotation systems · Collaborative software · Data analysis · Information science · Data modeling · Knowledge management · Database management systems · Time series databases distributed systems · Software architecture · Information visualization

1 Introduction

The prevalence and predominance of data acquisition hardware, such as smartphones, real-time sensors, Smart Home devices, and many other equipments composing the Internet of Things (IoT), has been a major factor in the explosive growth of data that we see today. While in 2016 the annual rate of data generation and traffic was at 1.2 zettabytes per year, it is projected that this rate will increase to 3.3 zettabytes per year by 2021[1]. To generate meaning from large collections of data, systems for analysis,

---

[1] https://www.cisco.com/c/en/us/solutions/collateral/service-provider/visual-networking-index-vni/vni-hyperconnectivity-wp.html.

© Springer Nature Switzerland AG 2020
S. Hammoudi et al. (Eds.): DATA 2019, CCIS 1255, pp. 59–82, 2020.
https://doi.org/10.1007/978-3-030-54595-6_4

automation, monitoring and anomaly detection have been developed. Human analysts can use these systems to easily explore and refine these data sets under a myriad of criteria, leading to the discovery of new segments of knowledge and relationships.

In many cases, the collected data is only useful if observations are made not to a single data point, but to sets of ordered data points over discrete, non-uniform time intervals, constituting time series [32]. Time series data can be found in almost every aspect of human life: medical diagnosis based on Electroencephalograms (EEGs) and Electrocardiograms (ECGs), financial technical analysis, monitoring and prediction of meteorological or natural occurrences, and many others.

Various analysis software solutions were developed to acquire, store and display time series data to a group of collaborating users, enabling the visual discovery of meaningful patterns or anomalies in multivariate data sets. The Artemis platform [6] is a fully-fledged server and web application that displays physiological data streams collected from patients waiting for care in the emergency department. Papers like [19] and [32] implement a similar web platform with the goal of enabling decision support for diagnosis based on physiological patient data. Other works focus on biomedical and healthcare time series data streams from ECGs terminals [3], prediction of high-frequency yet volatile financial time series data [16], and many other use cases.

While time series in themselves are highly capable of representing a measurement over time, their meaning is not directly conveyed. Human or machine observers require the assistance of appended metadata to create this unit of shared knowledge. This concept of a data annotation has been applied in a wide scope of domains as a way to critique the data, represent a memory aid, highlight an important segment, describe a taxonomy [26], or circumvent rigid records to express additional data that was not originally envisioned in the input data set [20]. Based on this, there is sufficient evidence available that shows that the usage of annotations in analysis platforms enables a more adequate decision-making process [24]. Through the use of annotations, the analysis system provides a versatile collaborative workflow for building chunks of knowledge. In [15] the authors propose a software solution where clinicians can explore biomedical time series and annotate segments of interest. In [19,20,32], the respective authors implement a system that stores data from real-time physiological streams and annotations made by analysts at remote locations.

While the phenomenon of increased metrification has led to a higher volume of data processed at the business level, this data is growing so fast that it is becoming progressively harder to expeditiously analyze and derive value from it. The previously mentioned domains typically produce large quantities of time series, which can often lead to data entropy and visual pollution that substantially increase the complexity and difficulty of analytical tasks, as well as demand higher development and financial costs. Therefore, modern analysis systems should be capable of handling massive data sets of time series and annotations at architectural, storage and visual levels. However, existing time series analysis systems have multiple shortcomings in this regard: **i)** these systems tendentially fail to implement distributed techniques like replication and partitioning to improve *availability* of the service; **ii)** although these systems use relational data management models that can persist large data sets, these models may not be the most efficient at querying time series while preserving atomicity of the knowledge-base; and

iii) time series line graphs in the Cartesian coordinate system, the most commonly used visualization for temporal data in these systems, can present a multitude of interpretation issues in highly heterogeneous domains, where a high number of time series fill up too much of the available visual space or compete with each other by tracing the same trajectories. Note that, throughout this paper, we quantify a massive time series data set as at least a dozen terabytes or more of series in uncompressed TSV files, holding over one million data points. As more and more series are collected from multiple data sources, the system should scale accordingly.

This paper extends on the work performed in [7], where we proposed a platform and a web application for collaborative time series analysis and listed the specific tools and techniques that were employed for it. In this extended paper we study and compare a wider set of architectural, data management and visualization approaches that can be applied to implement a highly *available* and *consistent* time series analysis and annotation system, as well as describe how to maximize said approaches at the implementation level. Additional approaches are listed, including series storage methods backed by column stores, techniques for modeling and storing annotation versions, and visualization technologies. Furthermore, we perform a benchmark study of read/write performance for a set of data stores that support time series, with the goal of discovering the most scalable and cost-efficient candidate.

2 Approaches

2.1 Architecture

Among various metrics that can be used to measure the efficiency of a system, two can be highlighted: *Availability*, which measures how long a system is accessible by clients; and *Consistency*, which measures how long every part of the system is synchronized, so that different requests to separate data stores will not return inconsistent data. A lack of *Consistency* does not affect *Availability*, but *Availability* mechanisms like replication make *Consistency* harder to maintain [36]. The Consistency, Availability and Partition tolerance (CAP) theorem [13] is an essential theorem in distributed systems that outlines how every system can only guarantee two out of three properties, *Consistency, Availability* and *Partition Tolerance*. An extension to the CAP theorem, the PACELC theorem [1], suggests that network partitioning is inevitable, and as such there is another trade-off between *Consistency* and *Latency*. Two different architectures can be outlined, respectively matching the analysis and the monitoring workflows: **i)** focus on *Consistency*: the system should propagate updates to the knowledge base in an atomic manner, prioritizing strong writes into the platform and synchronizing reads from other users to catch the latest updates without overriding or corrupting data; and **ii)** focus on *Latency*: the system should allow analysts to discover alarming events as close as possible to the moment they are measured, prioritizing fast reads. Therefore, an optimal architectural approach for an analysis system is one that, under the CAP theorem, follows the Consistency + Availability (C+A) model, and under the PACELC theorem, follows the Availability + Latency over Consistency (E+L) architecture for time series and the Consistency + Availability over Latency (E+C) architecture for the remaining data, preferring *eventual-consistency* and low latency in the acquisition of raw series but *strong-consistency* when inserting or updating knowledge.

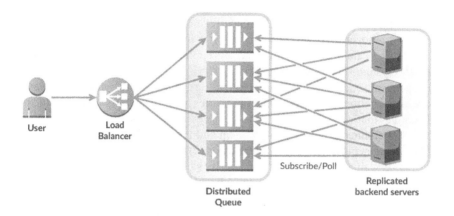

Fig. 1. Load balancing strategy with queued requests.

It is our belief that distributing processes and ensuring consistency across multiple servers should be a fundamental requirement of analysis systems, especially when dealing with data sets that often come with high cardinality such as time series. These systems are only considered efficient and scalable when they are capable of maintaining a synchronized view of a continuously-growing data set for multiple users at an acceptable response time and for the majority of its lifespan. To achieve this, both [6] and [38] have built a modular backend architecture that manages multiple independent processing adapters, using IBM InfoSphere[2]. The architecture automatically adapts to the increasing number of patients connected to the system, but no specific distributed techniques are mentioned. In [32] the author leverages an event-driven model where any component can subscribe to any activities in the system under a publish-subscribe pattern. However, the author mentions that there is no load-balancing of components, so the platform could run into *Availability* issues when concurrently used by multiple users. The platform described in [19] contains a Hypertext Transfer Protocol (HTTP) backend server with a Create, Read, Update and Delete (CRUD) interface using the Representational State Transfer (REST) protocol [10]. The communication channel between a web application and the relational database, where time series are stored, is made possible through this REST Application Programming Interface (API). Although this platform leverages modern web technologies, the authors also mention that, for massive amounts of time series, there is a considerable delay between acquiring new data and displaying it in the frontend.

The backend system should be capable of maintaining high-performance over multiple simultaneous requests and of handling failures to guarantee as much uptime as possible. For this, the backend application could be replicated over multiple servers/containers

---

[2] https://www.ibm.com/analytics/information-server.

whose single point of entry is a load balancer unit, as shown in Fig. 1. Because a load balancer alone does not typically provide queuing of requests, all requests will continue to be redirected to the servers even if they are under strain. To solve this, a distributed message queue is leveraged to keep the subsequent requests in a First-In-First-Out (FIFO) queue. The load balancer is set with a Least Connections balancing policy, where requests are redirected to the queue with the least amount queued requests. Queues are then replicated in order to adapt to increased or decreased simultaneous usage and to provide a failover measure. Then, backend servers subscribe to a queue and only poll requests when they are free to process it.

2.2 Time Series Storage

A wide majority of the previously mentioned time series analysis systems implement persistence logic with a single relational database node. The usage of a Relational Database Management System (RDBMS) enables the optimal storage and indexing of time series with a wide variety of data types (e.g. geospatial locations) and the modeling of a strong relational schema, but the question of wherever these RDBMSs are the most efficient choice for storing time series when compared with other, more recent technologies is left unanswered.

While many RDBMSs such as PostgreSQL[3] already support temporal segments, these do not integrate temporal data *rollup* procedures that sort and summarize time series under data views with decreased detail. These procedures would allow queries to be made to the data set without knowing the range ahead of time and without needing to scan a massive amount of records individually. In the last few years there has been a surge in time series databases with *rollup* mechanisms that employ RDBMSs as a backend, inheriting their flexible data model, their battle-tested reliability and performance, and their ecosystem of open-source extensions. One such database is TimescaleDB[4], built with PostgreSQL. A few studies suggest that TimescaleDB has favorable performance for both insertions and queries when directly compared with other database systems like InfluxDB[5] [12], Cassandra[6] [17] and PostgreSQL [27]. However, the majority of these benchmarks are written by the authors of TimescaleDB and have not been independently reviewed.

Although a strong relational schema for time series could be a positive feature for aggregate queries that require time series, annotations and users all-in-one, [22] and [29] suggest that using a traditional RDBMS for time series management can result in less than optimal performance at scale when compared with Time Series Database Management Systems (TSDBMSs). TSDBMSs index timestamps as primary identifiers and perform temporal *rollups* to improve query speed. Since the early 2000s there have been multiple attempts at implementing TSDBMSs, but only the most recent generation of open-source TSDBMSs have been deliberately developed to handle massive amounts of time series, responding to modern requirements of data processing [22].

---

[3] https://www.postgresql.org/.

[4] https://www.timescale.com/.

[5] https://www.influxdata.com/.

[6] http://cassandra.apache.org/.

In [2] the authors evaluate the performance of various TSDBMSs such as InfluxDB, Druid[7], OpenTSDB[8], ElasticSearch[9], MonetDB[10] and Prometheus[11], all of which are implemented using a Log-structured Merge (LSM) tree data structure [31] that specializes in storing values indexed by unique keys. The authors concluded that both Druid and InfluxDB offered the best long-term storage functionality, but when compared with RDBMSs, TSDBMSs have a more limited data model and a lack of features such as constraints, data validation and fault-tolerance mechanisms.

The biggest issue with all the previously mentioned TSDBMSs is the lack of clustering and partitioning techniques that allow them to scale and remain highly *available* as the data set continues to grow. This can be mitigated by using a Column-oriented Database Management System (CDBMS) data store geared for scaling like Cassandra, an open-source, distributed NoSQL CDBMS that is also based on a LSM tree backend. The benchmarks performed in [23] for HBase[12] and Cassandra showed that while both are linearly scalable for native writes, both present lower performance for aggregate temporal queries of large volumes of data. To address this exact issue, a number of time series databases were implemented on top of scalable data stores like Cassandra and HBase, such as Blueflood[13], KairosDB[14] and Databus[15]. In [14], the authors suggest that KairosDB is able to fulfill near-linear scalability, load balancing, clustering and reliability requirements better than OpenTSDB and Databus. The previously mentioned benchmark in [2] also studied the features of KairosDB and Blueflood, and while the required time series roll-up and aggregation algorithms are fully supported by these tools, the authors concluded that TSDBMSs should still be capable of delivering better performance overall.

Based solely on the studies mentioned in this section, modern LSM tree TSDBMSs databases are the best candidates for fully-featured and efficient querying of massive amounts of historical data, albeit lacking *availability* mechanisms built-in. InfluxDB shows over multiple studies to have both the smallest impact on disk storage and the lowest latency when querying long-term historical time series, which fits the intended use case. However, InfluxDB also comes with a few drawbacks when compared to other database systems, such as the limited data model. To further validate our preference for InfluxDB, we have selected the data stores that have shown the better results overall in the explored research, namely InfluxDB, PostgreSQL, MySQL and KairosDB (Cassandra), and carried out a performance benchmark study for these, covered in the Evaluation section.

---

[7] http://druid.io/.

[8] http://opentsdb.net/.

[9] https://www.elastic.co/products/elasticsearch.

[10] https://www.monetdb.org/.

[11] https://prometheus.io/.

[12] https://hbase.apache.org/.

[13] http://blueflood.io/.

[14] https://kairosdb.github.io/.

[15] https://github.com/deanhiller/databus.

2.3   Annotation Storage

TSDBMSs are unable to structure relationships, making them unwieldy to use for storing an ontology where various related entities are commonly queried together. Similarly, CDBMSs provide more a distributed solution by weakening relations between two separate entities/tables. With this, the relational database presents itself as the strongest candidate for structuring strong relationships between annotations and collaborators. All of the studied time series analysis solutions that provide annotation support take advantage of RDBMSs to model a strong relationship between annotations and other entities that are often requested simultaneously (such as user data).

Benchmark studies on the performance of open-source RDBMSs, such as [2,23,35], promote PostgreSQL as being the most feature-complete and performant option. PostgreSQL is ideal when prioritizing *strong-consistency* due to its robust Multi-version Concurrency Control (MVCC) model [30] that values Atomicity, Consistency, Isolation and Durability(ACID). MySQL[16] commonly reports faster reads and writes than PostgreSQL, but it achieves this by prioritizing *Availability* over *Consistency* in its design[17].

In any annotation task, a user is given the possibility to observe and propose meaning over data, and other users should naturally be able to discuss it and evolve it until an agreement between collaborators is reached. Each step should be historically recorded as *versions*, so that unsanctioned changes can be rolled-back at any point in time [20]. Although traditional databases do not support versioning directly, there are various models for storing versioned data that can be implemented while using these databases.

Snodgrass [37] proposed extensions to the SQL language in order to allow entities to have a preserved historical state within their records. This approach minimizes the need to create separate tables to store historical data, but also leads to many more disadvantages, since the appending of multiple versions into a single table will cause queries to go over an exponentially higher number of records that scale both vertically (as the number of separate entities increases) and horizontally (as the number of versions of each entity increases) [5].

In order to tackle the drawbacks of this approach, the historical data can instead be stored in separate versioning tables. This is similar to the event-sourcing pattern [11], where all application events, including updates and before-and-after snapshots, are stored in a append-only log [28]. This approach translates to higher-performant queries for both the current state of the data and for the historical data, but without compression mechanisms or expiration policies, it can gradually generate a large disk overhead. Another alternative model is one based on deltas [5], where each record in a versioning table contains only the contents of fields that were changed in that version. The contents of unchanged fields can be reconstructed by performing a theta join over all prior versions where those fields were last changed. Although this approach has a considerably lower impact on disk usage, it can be too cumbersome and slow to rebuild the contents of a version when dealing with highly-volatile entities.

---

[16] https://www.mysql.com/.

[17] https://wiki.postgresql.org/wiki/Why_PostgreSQL_Instead_of_MySQL:_Comparing_Reliability_and_Speed_in_2007.

Fig. 2. Timelion dashboard displaying multiple time series charts in simultaneous, from [7].

Overall, all of the listed approaches correspond to a storage vs efficiency trade-off. Any attempts at compressing the version data set, either by using version deltas or by compressing the data itself, will negatively affect query performance, while any attempts at improving query performance will negatively affect disk usage [4,21].

2.4 Time Series Visualization

In [18], the authors compared multiple visualization web toolkits such as Google Charts, JIT and Protovis, concluding that Protovis is the most versatile tool out of the tested ones, but did not include other, more recent visualization libraries like D3[18], plotly.js[19] and Dygraphs[20]. *WebPlotViz* [25] is a web-based tri-dimensional visualization application built with WebGL[21] and three.js[22], and while the 3D aspect is functional and innovative, WebGL performance degrades considerably as the amount of rendered data points increases. Both [19] and [32] implement a web application using Adobe Flash plugin technology to display real-time physiological streams from EEGs, but Flash is very taxing on memory, incompatible with most mobile devices, and will be discontinued in 2020[23]. Therefore, modern frontend tools should leverage Hypertext Markup Language (HTML) features and open-source JavaScript visualization libraries that enable the application to be cross-browser compatible in both desktop and mobile devices.

---

[18] https://d3js.org/.

[19] https://plot.ly/javascript/.

[20] http://dygraphs.com/.

[21] https://www.khronos.org/webgl/.

[22] https://threejs.org/.

[23] https://blogs.adobe.com/conversations/2011/11/flash-focus.html.

Most of the previously mentioned software solutions provide time series visualization within web applications. The most recent developments made to the web browser and JavaScript technologies, the near-universal availability of web browsers in the majority of computers and mobile devices, and the ubiquity in the way users are accustomed to interact with these, make the web platform a more attractive choice for the development of data science software.

In the commercial and open-source space, there are multiple dashboard tools for visualization of time series, such as *Timelion*[24], *Grafana*[25] and *Freeboard*[26], that implement both a shared-space model, where multiple time series co-exist in the same chart, and a split-space model, where series are displayed in separate charts, as shown in Fig. 2. In either of the two space distribution models, both graphs have perceptual thresholds directly correlated with the number of time series displayed simultaneously [8]: **i)** if the number of simultaneous time series on display in the same chart increases, it becomes exponentially harder to compare how these series act within the same segment of time; and **ii)** if the number of simultaneous charts increases, the amount of visual space required to display all the separate charts will also increase, often exceeding the available space within a view window.

2.5   Annotation Visualization

In [20], the proposed time series analysis system supports annotations as both waveform classifications, highlighting an area with a unique color that matches a category or meaning, and as textual notes, relating events outside of the data set. Open-source dashboard tools like *Timelion* and *Grafana* combine the two representations by implementing annotations as textual notes that are displayed in the chart as either vertical lines (for point annotations) or rectangular highlights (for ranged annotations), both occupying the full vertical area of the chart. These approaches match a data model where annotations are only attached to segments of time, but this is a limited model that lacks flexibility of expression since an annotation cannot be attached to only a subset of the series that are displayed in the same segment. As an attempt to solve this, in *TSPad* [33] annotations are freeform shapes that can be sketched around the intended series. Although this approach is readable by human collaborators, it also results in unstructured data that automated systems can only interpret, albeit unreliably, through the use of graphical parsing algorithms.

In other words, this issue must be solved at the data model level. Annotations could contain a set of annotated series that limit its scope in their segment. This set can also be left empty, denoting a global annotation for a segment of time that is identical to the previous approach. This way, annotations are logically connected with their series and can handle realistic scenarios of note-taking and commentary more appropriately. The digital medium allows annotations to be easily set up as contextual extensions of a series subset that can be modified over time without ever affecting the original data set.

To assist this data model, we propose a visual encoding of *snakes*, where annotations are rendered as arcs that follow the affected series' curves when inside the specified

---

[24] https://www.elastic.co/blog/timelion-timeline.

[25] https://grafana.com/.

[26] http://freeboard.io/.

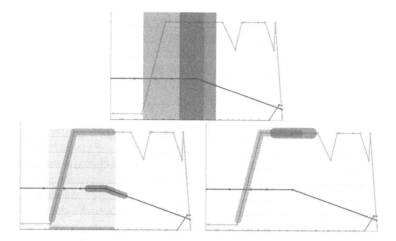

Fig. 3. Visual representation of annotations, from [7]. From top to bottom and left to right: i) two intersecting annotations in other time series visualization tools; ii) proposed annotation encoding, with two annotations intersecting in the same segment of time but not over the same series; iii) proposed annotation encoding, with two nested annotations intersecting in the same segment of time and over the same series.

segment of time, as shown in Fig. 3. *Snakes* will only trace over series that are associated with the annotation, leaving other series in the same segment uncovered. If an annotation affects more than one series in the same segment, multiple *snakes* are traced over all of the affected curves, and a polygonal overlay is painted in a way that vertically connects all *snakes* of the same annotation. With this, annotations can be attached to smaller areas of the chart while keeping the remaining vertical space clear from visual clutter.

As Fig. 3 also shows, when two annotations intersect over one another by overlapping on the same segment of time, two output encodings may occur: if the annotations are covering different series, the two *snakes* tracing over different curves will be sufficient to visually differentiate the two annotations; if the annotation are overlapping on the same series, one of the *snakes* assumes a wider radius in order to nest the other, keeping both in view and with clickable areas.

3   Implementation and Challenges

We developed a time series analysis web platform that handles common use cases for knowledge discovery, reviewing and sharing in an optimized manner. The end goal of this prototype is to iterate on existing analysis platforms and to leverage what we consider to be, at the time of writing, the most appropriate approaches and open-source tools for querying, storing and displaying time series and annotations, as discussed in the previous section. The backend system was implemented in Java 8[27] using various

---

[27] https://www.oracle.com/technetwork/java/javase/overview/java8-2100321.html.

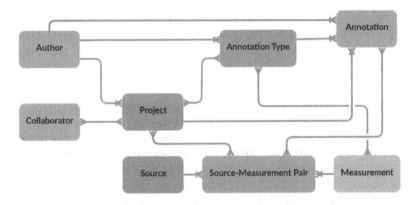

Fig. 4. Relational diagram of entities, from [7].

modules from the Spring Boot 2.0[28] stack. The web application was implemented in ReactJS[29], using TypeScript[30] as the primary programming language.

3.1 Data Model

The input data set is assumed to contain points from different series and from different data sources. The term *measurement* is used to describe a specific series and all of its meta-data, such as a name, a color and a data type (e.g. a number or a boolean state), and the term *source* is used to describe a data origin device. Each source can contain multiple measurements, and each measurement can exist in multiple sources, so every time series is uniquely identified by a source-measurement pair. If the input data set does not identify any point of supply or does not contain multiple measures, then the platform will accommodate the entire data set within a single data source or a single measurement respectively.

The designation of *ontology* is used in this paper to describe all of the entities that are generated from user input and that compose the knowledge base of the platform, such as annotations, annotation types and user profiles. Measurement and source definitions are also included as part of the ontology, although the actual series points are not. To separate annotations at the contextual level, establishing an annotation goal over a subset of the available time series, all annotations are contained within *projects*. Projects are essentially scopes of analysis that are shared with a group of collaborators, restricting them to a segment of time and a set of series data points that match a specified query, and to a limited number of annotation types that can be used.

Figure 4 shows how ontology entities relate to one another. Note that while projects, annotations and annotation-types have a set of users related to them, data sources and

---

[28] https://spring.io/projects/spring-boot.

[29] https://reactjs.org/.

[30] https://www.typescriptlang.org/.

measurements do not, as these two are automatically modeled at the system level based on the input time series data. Additionally, while this diagram separates *Author* from *Collaborator*, when stored in a RDBMS these two entities are unified under the same *User* entity.

$$A = (t_1, t_2, p, c, u, txt, \{s_1, s_2, ..., s_n\}) \tag{1}$$

Annotations are expressed as in 1, where: t is a timestamp in the ISO-8601 format and in the Coordinated Universal Time (UTC) standard, so t_1 and t_2 are respectively the start and end of a segment of time; p is the parent project; c is the parent category or type; u is the author of the annotation; txt is a free-text field with unstructured notes; and the s-set is the annotated time series within the specified segment, identified by their source-measurement pairs. The proposed representation enforces a set of common fields that simplify searchability and versioning, and allows annotations to be both readable by human observers and interpretable by machines for indexing and data mining purposes. The starting and the ending points can be set to the same timestamp, fundamentally representing a point annotation instead of a region. The annotation type is taken from a global repository of types, enforcing a common semantic across different projects, series and segments of time. Annotation types also have a set of constraints that restricts the segment type (point or range) and annotated measurements of child annotations.

All entities are modeled within the codebase with the Hibernate[31] Object-Relational Mapping (ORM), using both the Java Persistence API (JPA) and Hibernate API to describe tables, indexes, columns and relations. This introduces type safety, improves readability, and enable features such as Integrated Development Environment (IDE) support and debugging through the Java compiler to facilitate maintenance over long development cycles.

3.2 Data Management

The implemented solution leverages a granular persistence model [9] that takes advantage of both a strong relational schema and a high-performance time series database. Our benchmarks, explored in the Evaluation section, showed that InfluxDB has a smaller disk impact and a higher query speed for long-term historical time series, deeming it as the most suitable choice for an E+L architecture. Likewise, the studied research has consistently shown that PostgreSQL has great performance and a strong model for consistent reads and writes, making it the perfect fit for an E+C architecture. Furthermore, because multiple aspects of the platform require name searches, PostgreSQL's built-in functionality of text vector indexing for full-text search is advantageous, as it enables name searches within paginated queries that are more performant than regex matches while mitigating the added complexity of deploying and managing consistency of an inverted-index database like Elasticsearch or Solr[32].

This polyglot architecture means that the overall traffic workload is distributed between two independent units of storage depending on what is being queried. However, because the client can simultaneously request data types that are split between these two units, the overall architecture has to ensure that these queries can be executed

---

[31] http://hibernate.org/.

[32] http://lucene.apache.org/solr/.

asynchronously to avoid bottlenecks. In order to enable queries for time series by their relation with annotations in a way that reduces dependency on the ontology database, we include linked annotation IDs, as well as their respective annotation-type IDs and project IDs, in the annotated time series points as indexed tags. A central backend or broker unit is placed between the requesting user and the two databases to enforce the data access logic, managing links between the two databases and concealing from the end-user the real location of the data. In other words, while the ontology data set has *strong-consistency*, the time series data set has links that are *eventually-consistent*.

After an ontology update completes successfully, annotation links are added to (or removed from) affected series points in InfluxDB to match the latest ontology state. However, if two concurrent requests with overlapping series were to be sent, because these requests cannot be made atomically to a single field but rather read and perform changes over the same state of the series, one request would inadvertently discard the changes from the other and cause a race condition. To solve this, all InfluxDB write requests are placed in a single FIFO queue, providing an ordered channel of write proposals. Each proposal naturally fetches the previous changes made to the affected series and merges them with new ones. Read-only queries are not queued and can happen in parallel with writes. This approach increases the inconsistency window of InfluxDB, but it is guaranteed that both data stores are eventually converged on a synchronized state without any data loss.

Every annotation, annotation-type and project is versioned, allowing collaborators to revert unsanctioned changes. Historical records are stored in separate revision tables, emulating the append-only logs of event-sourcing architectures. Versioning logic is implemented through Hibernate Envers[33], which automatically orchestrates the generation of revision tables based on the data model. Versions are created within the same transaction as insertions and updates, so as to avoid opening an inconsistency window where an entity is updated without the previous snapshot being available in the version table.

3.3 Architecture

Figure 5 shows the implemented architecture. Every request made in the frontend layer is sent through HTTP to the load balancer module and arrives at a REST API in the backend layer. This REST API gateway enables additional input or output units to be added to the architecture, independent from the visualization stack. The entire architecture is deployed using Docker Swarm[34], which enables an infrastructure where each unit can be distributed between nodes or containers. This is particularly helpful in enabling the proposed distributed system and facilitating system orchestration, as both the number of distributed queues in RabbitMQ[35] and the number of backend servers can automatically increase or decrease as the platform scales and more traffic is detected. To reduce the latency of requests that fetch or require the same entities, a Redis[36] cache is deployed

---

[33] https://hibernate.org/orm/envers/.

[34] https://docs.docker.com/engine/swarm/.

[35] http://www.rabbitmq.com.

[36] https://redis.io/.

with a Least Recently Used (LRU) eviction policy. The client connection with Redis is made through the Spring Data Redis library[37], which already provides functionality to serialize the ORM entities from and to cached objects.

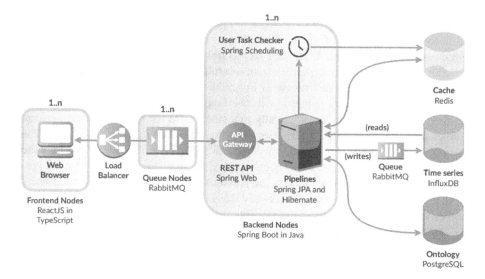

Fig. 5. Platform architecture. Backend and queue nodes can be replicated on-demand to accommodate intensive workloads, reproducing the load balancing strategy shown in Fig. 1. A frontend node is launched for each user/browser session.

Every operation in the platform, other than the login request, is authenticated. The platform can be configured to either: **i)** store passwords hashed in BCrypt [34] and match these with passwords that are sent in subsequent login requests; or **ii)** link the user in this platform to a user in a Lightweight Directory Access Protocol (LDAP) server, and use the authentication process of the LDAP to validate the credentials. After a successful login, the JJWT library[38] is used to generate a session token based on JSON Web Tokens (JWTs). All JWTs have an expiration date, to prevent a man-in-the-middle attacker from indefinitely using a captured token.

The backend server is best viewed as a batch of processing pipelines, where requests go through a sequential order of stages: authentication; payload deserialization; validation; conversion of the request to a valid query or procedure; and serialization of results while concealing extraneous data. Any request or response body that passes through the REST API is encoded in JavaScript Object Notation (JSON), so these can be deserialized to a binary object in Java using the Jackson[39] library. The validation stage evaluates insertion or update request payloads, checking mandatory fields and invalid characters and testing relationship constraints based on the data model. For an annotation A, a

---

[37] https://spring.io/projects/spring-data-redis.
[38] https://github.com/jwtk/jjwt.
[39] https://github.com/FasterXML/jackson.

parent annotation type T, a parent project P, and a source-measurement pair SM with a measurement M, the relationship constraints are: **i)** A is annotating SM, which is queried by P; **ii)** A is annotating SM, therefore is annotating M, which is allowed by T; **iii)** A is annotating a segment (point or range) that is allowed by T; and **iv)** A is of type T, which is allowed to be used in P.

Depending on the amount of changes to contents and entity relationships that are being committed, update transactions to the ontology database can take a long time to complete. To expedite the processing of changes, every update or version rollback is committed within an asynchronous thread. The pipeline simultaneously processes the request and returns a simulated snapshot of the results to the user, which matches how the entity will look like in subsequent queries after the changes have been fully committed.

When two or more users are working simultaneously over the same entities, one user will inevitably run into a situation where the last queried version of an entity could be outdated, as it has already been updated by another user. Without a way to detect stale data, the database can allow the second user to submit changes based on an outdated snapshot, potentially discarding changes from other users. To enforce a sequential workflow without conflicts, an optimistic-locking policy is implemented. This policy dictates that requesting users should always provide the last-modified date of the entity they propose changes to, which acts as the version field. If the provided date and the last-modified date of the respective entity in the database do not match, the update should be canceled and the user should re-fetch the entity and manually merge their changes.

Through the use of Spring JPA library[40] and Hibernate, the backend server connects to PostgreSQL in an agnostic manner. Spring provides a set of database-agnostic Spring components called *repositories* that allow the specification of queries using Java Persistence Query Language (JPQL), a SQL-like language that is translated to the SQL variant used the chosen data store when the backend is deployed. This abstracted connection enables a hotswap-like architecture that adapts to a configured relational database, and can be swapped at any point. Spring does not contain a client for InfluxDB, so this had to be implemented using the official InfluxDB Java driver[41]. Series queries are modeled as a structured object in order to expose the query capabilities of InfluxDB to the end user while enforcing the custom logic of annotation linking. Additionally, this query object enforces an uniform structure that can be traversed by both backend and frontend systems, so the backend can check for unbounded parameters to prevent injection attacks while the frontend can display the query in a criteria builder User Interface (UI). Users send this structured query object to the REST API serialized in JSON, and once validated, the query object is converted into a valid InfluxQL query.

3.4 Visualization

Although the existing frontend applications that provide user-configurable dashboard workspaces, such as *Timelion* and *Grafana*, could be connected with our input data set in order to display it, these do not support custom-made annotation encodings, such

---

[40] http://spring.io/projects/spring-data-jpa.

[41] https://github.com/influxdata/influxdb-java.

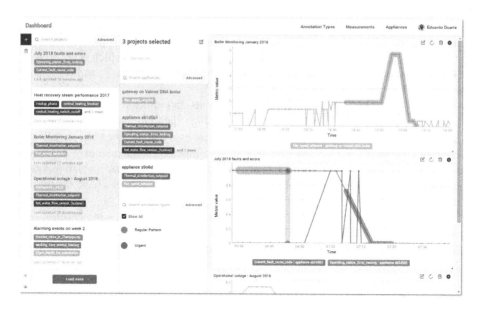

Fig. 6. Dashboard with three projects and two sources selected, from [7]. Note that the source identified as "appliance eb1d5b1" contains measurements from two separate projects, as these are merged when displayed on the source list.

as the proposed *snakes* visualization, nor the inclusion of business logic, such as the previously described relationship constraints and structured series queries. Therefore, a custom frontend application with a similar dashboard interface was implemented.

This interface, using Ant Design components[42], leverages the UI paradigm of panels and windows, displaying projects, queried sources and their measurements, visible annotation types, and chart windows simultaneously, as seen in Fig. 6. Collaborators can modify query criterias while keeping the series and annotations always in view. The user can select a project or multiple through *ctrl-clicks* or *shift-clicks*, and the interface will display the combined data from all selected projects, merging the lists of sources, measurements and annotation types and spawning a chart window per project. Any chart window can be moved, resized, or closed, the latter of which will de-select the project.

The implemented application is composed of multiple interface modules that can be individually re-rendered when their data is updated. Redux[43] is used to handle application state and reactive propagation of data throughout relevant modules, while axios[44] is used as a HTTP client for the implemented REST API.

$$Y = v_a + (X - t_a) / (t_b - t_a) \cdot (v_b - v_a) \tag{2}$$

---

[42] https://ant.design.

[43] https://redux.js.org/.

[44] https://github.com/axios/axios.

Line charts are implemented with the Dygraphs library[45]. Dygraphs renders all series, x and y axis, and labels on top of a HTML 2D Canvas[46], which exposes enough functionality to paint the desired *snakes*. Every visible data point is matched with the timestamps of annotations in order to find the exact start and end coordinates in the Document Object Model (DOM)[47]. When these timestamps are set to a x coordinate without any actual data points, the y value is determined through interpolation. By using the previous data point a and the next data point b, with timestamps t_a and t_b and values v_a and v_b respectively, (2) can be used to obtain an interpolated Y value for an annotation that starts, ends, or is a point in X. Once the starting and ending points have been determined, the *snake* can be drawn by tracing a line over these and over all of the real points in-between. When the current zoomed view does not display the starting and/or ending points of an annotation, the first and/or last visible data points act as stand-ins.

4 Evaluation

4.1 Performance Testing of Databases for Time Series Storage

Existing research on time series storage technologies has been instrumental in reducing the number of candidates for time series storage to just four: InfluxDB (TSDBMS), KairosDB (CDBMS), PostgreSQL and MySQL (RDBMSs). These four typically show high-performance in the surveyed benchmarks, and according to these studies, have varying levels of advantages over the others depending on the desired use case. Whereas RDBMSs can provide an ACID-compliant option, TSDBMSs and CDBMSs might deliver higher read/write speeds and, in the case of KairosDB, provide built-in clustering support.

To refine this selection and discover the best candidate for the purposes of long-term storage and analysis, we benchmarked these tools using a multivariate Heating, Ventilation and Air-Conditioning (HVAC) data set, collected from 1000 DNA boilers over the course of 1.3 years. All tests were executed using the same deployment conditions: a single server node with a 2.50 GHz Quad-Core processor and 16 GB RAM memory. MySQL was configured with the InnoDB storage engine, and KairosDB was tested with 2 clusters and a replication factor of 3. To test write performance, insertions used batches of 200,000 points, which is a sufficiently large window to allow a massive data set to be quickly committed without exceeding the machine resources or exhausting the connection pool. Every query is filtered by a segment of time that is never changed and three source-measurement pairs P_1, P_2 and P_3, of which: **i)** P_1 and P_2 have the same measurement M with numeric values; **ii)** P_2 and P_3 have the same source S; and **iii)** P_3 contains state values. The evaluated queries are as follows: *1)* get all three pairs (no filters); *2)* get the same three pairs, but $v_{P_1} > 4$, $v_{P_2} \leq 2$, and $v_{P_3} = true$; *3)* get the same three pairs, but all pairs are globally filtered with $v > 4$ (returning only numeric series P_1 and P_2 that match this condition). All of these queries were executed over twenty times for each database, and observed for data sets with ten thousand (10,000), a hundred thousand (100,000), and a million (1,000,000) points.

---

[45] http://dygraphs.com/.

[46] https://developer.mozilla.org/en-US/docs/Web/API/Canvas_API.

[47] https://developer.mozilla.org/en-US/docs/Web/API/Document_Object_Model/Introduction.

The benchmark results in Table 1 show that CPU usage and elapsed query speed do not differ severely for smaller data sets (Fig. 7). However, as the data set grows and reaches a hundred thousand data points or more, InfluxDB outperforms all other databases in both query speed and CPU requirements. Additionally, the request time and CPU usage of PostgreSQL, MySQL and KairosDB increase drastically, making these the least scalable options. KairosDB trades-off querying performance with the ability to cluster and increase *availability* of data, but the performance difference is too major to consider it over InfluxDB.

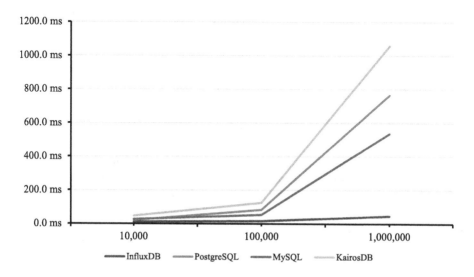

Fig. 7. Average request time observed during reads.

Table 1. Average request time and CPU usage observed for the three queries.

DB	Q	10,000 points		100,000 points		1,000,000 points	
		Time	CPU	Time	CPU	Time	CPU
InfluxDB	1	8 ms	0.24%	16 ms	0.52%	62 ms	2.55%
	2	16 ms	0.22%	15 ms	0.51%	47 ms	1.95%
	3	9 ms	0.19%	16 ms	0.41%	31 ms	1.53%
PGSQL	1	16 ms	0.69%	125 ms	4.93%	984 ms	97.91%
	2	31 ms	1.02%	78 ms	5.04%	859 ms	112.93%
	3	16 ms	0.08%	47 ms	3.34%	453 ms	61.70%
MySQL	1	31 ms	1.04%	62 ms	3.08%	609 ms	35.48%
	2	32 ms	1.22%	53 ms	2.27%	485 ms	33.65%
	3	15 ms	1.06%	47 ms	2.62%	516 ms	46.08%
KairosDB	1	49 ms	2.84%	138 ms	26.01%	1.21 s	125.61%
	2	50 ms	2.67%	121 ms	27.46%	1.01 s	162.15%
	3	43 ms	3.94%	116 ms	14.98%	956 ms	118.32%

The benchmark results in Table 2 show that InfluxDB has a higher throughput for insertions and better on-disk compression than other databases, making it more ideal for long-term storage. PostgreSQL, MySQL and KairosDB took considerably longer than InfluxDB to insert the full data set in batches, making InfluxDB also the better candidate for highly volatile data sets that collect new series points at a rapid rate. The nearest competitor of InfluxDB in terms of disk overhead is KairosDB, but while this strong disk compression affects the read performance of KairosDB, InfluxDB still delivers fast reads due to its memory-cached aggregated *rollups*, which conversely is also the leading factor in its high RAM memory requirement.

Table 2. Average insertion time, disk usage and RAM memory usage observed during writes.

DB	10,000 points			100,000 points		
	Time	Disk	RAM	Time	Disk	RAM
InfluxDB	862.4 ms	0.04 MB	139.3 MB	3.021 s	3.66 MB	298.9 MB
PGSQL	9.468 s	6.3 MB	25.62 MB	1.634 min	53.7 MB	26.93 MB
MySQL	1.381 min	42 MB	28.1 MB	9.128 min	172.6 MB	103.8 MB
KairosDB	15.22 s	0.63 MB	1.18 GB	2.755 min	42.26 MB	1.18 GB

	1,000,000 points		
DB	Time	Disk	RAM
InfluxDB	21.57 s	17.93 MB	1.64 GB
PGSQL	15.26 min	1119 MB	29.43 MB
MySQL	1.942 h	1.56 GB	186.6 MB
KairosDB	25.68 min	65.96 MB	1.18 GB

4.2 Performance Testing of Monoglot vs Polyglot Architectures

The previous benchmark motivated the usage of InfluxDB for long-term storage of time series, but because it would be too impractical to store our strongly-coupled ontology in a time series database, we instead store it in PostgreSQL, employing a polyglot architecture. Although one of our major goals was to build a system with *strong-consistency*, as the granularity of data increases and more data stores are used, *consistency* becomes harder to attain. By reducing this granularity and storing the entire data set in a single ACID-compliant database, while modeling relationships of time series with annotations without an ad-hoc linking mechanism, *consistency* can be maintained more easily. With this, we decided to examine how would the implemented system behave and perform if both the ontology and the time series data set were stored in the same RDBMS. The goal of these tests was not to solely compare the raw performance of both data stores, which is already covered in the previous test, but rather to potentially recognize if the performance drop from PostgreSQL could still be an acceptable trade-off to gain in reads, where series and annotations could be polled simultaneously through joins, and in writes, where one single transaction would propagate changes to annotations and series atomically.

The deployment conditions for these tests were identical to the ones listed in the previous test, but rather than sending queries directly to the target databases, the queries are sent to the backend server, bypassing the load balancer and the InfluxDB write request FIFO queue. The backend then detects the required data types and collects it from the respective data stores in a single transaction. Every query is filtered by the same segment of time and the same three source-measurement pairs P_1, P_2 and P_3 from the previous test. Over 500 annotations were added to random series. The evaluated queries are as follows: A) get all three pairs, but P_1 is filtered by an annotation (returning only points of P_1 that are annotated by said annotation); B) get the same three pairs, but P_2 is filtered by a project (returning only points of P_2 that are queried by said project); C) get the same three pairs, but all pairs are globally filtered by an annotation (returning only points of P_1, P_2 and P_3 that are annotated by said annotation). Note that all of

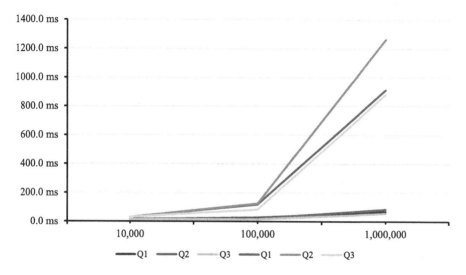

Fig. 8. Average request time observed during reads in the two data management models. Purple lines (first 3 in the legend) correspond to the polyglot model and orange lines (last 3 in the legend) to the monoglot model. (Color figure online)

Table 3. Average request time and CPU usage observed in different data management models.

Model	Q	10,000 points Time	10,000 points CPU	100,000 points Time	100,000 points CPU	1,000,000 points Time	1,000,000 points CPU
Polyglot *InfluxDB + PGSQL*	A	15.4 ms	0.29%	28.2 ms	0.56%	68.6 ms	3.82%
	B	19.2 ms	0.36%	22.0 ms	0.61%	84.6 ms	5.33%
	C	15.6 ms	0.23%	16.0 ms	0.56%	56.4 ms	3.81%
Monoglot *PGSQL only*	A	31.4 ms	0.83%	118.6 ms	6.72%	912.6 ms	128.60%
	B	31 ms	1.22%	124.4 ms	7.56%	1.26 s	143.68%
	C	31.4 ms	0.90%	84.2 ms	5.15%	881.4 ms	119.69%

these queries will require non-series data to be fetched, so in the polyglot strategy both InfluxDB and PostgreSQL will be queried, properly evaluating the effectiveness of this architecture when compared to a monoglot one.

The benchmark results in Table 3 show that the added value of using solely PostgreSQL for the entire data set does not balance out its drastic drop in performance for massive amounts of time series (Fig. 8). Much like in the previous test, although there is only a negligible difference in reads for smaller data sets when compared with the polyglot model, as the data set grows the read performance of PostgreSQL drops dramatically, and querying both data stores separately is still more efficient. Moreover, query B is more computationally expensive for PostgreSQL, as it performs two left-joins in order to fetch parent projects of annotations, whereas InfluxDB performs similarly to queries A and C as it relies on links alone. With this, the polyglot architecture continues to be the better option for scalable systems.

5 Conclusion

In this paper we presented and tested a set of architectural, data modeling, data management and visualization approaches, and nominated a few of these as the most cost-effective approaches to achieve the following goals: **i)** high-performant workflows in both the frontend and backend, adaptable to any data irrespective of the domain; **ii)** improved analysis tools that leverage both the shared-space model and the split-space model and reduce the number of trade-offs that come from picking only one of the two; **iii)** flexible visual representation of annotations that attach meaning to isolated segments of data and co-exist with other unaffected metrics; **iv)** streamlined framework of reliable contributions that are strongly validated and historically recorded; and **v)** scalability to handle both massive data sets and heavy traffic. All of these features combined facilitate analytical and knowledge-building tasks by human collaborators, improving productivity and saving them time. By taking advantage of the acquired know-how, the work presented in this paper serves as a foundation to develop more mature time series analysis software.

Furthermore, we validated these approaches by implementing them within a distributed architecture and a web application. Additional modules can easily be connected with the REST API to input additional time series or annotations from sensors or real-time data streams, introducing the ability to stream real time critical data that requires a timely analysis. This REST API could also be used to collect produced annotations and train machine-learning models with them to recognize similar patterns in other locations of the data set.

Acknowledgements. The present study was developed in the scope of the Smart Green Homes Project [POCI-01-0247-FEDER-007678], a co-promotion between Bosch Termotecnologia S.A. and the University of Aveiro. It is financed by Portugal 2020 under the Competitiveness and Internationalization Operational Program, and by the European Regional Development Fund.

References

1. Abadi, D.: Consistency tradeoffs in modern distributed database system design: cap is only part of the story. Computer **45**(2), 37–42 (2012)

2. Bader, A., Kopp, O., Falkenthal, M.: Survey and comparison of open source time series databases. In: Mitschang, B., et al. (eds.) Datenbanksysteme für Business, Technologie und Web (BTW 2017) - Workshopband, pp. 249–268. Gesellschaft für Informatik e.V, Bonn (2017)

3. Bar-Or, A., Healey, J., Kontothanassis, L., Thong, J.M.V.: Biostream: a system architecture for real-time processing of physiological signals. In: The 26th Annual International Conference of the IEEE Engineering in Medicine and Biology Society, vol. 2, pp. 3101–3104, September 2004. https://doi.org/10.1109/IEMBS.2004.1403876

4. Bhardwaj, A., et al.: Datahub: Collaborative data science & dataset version management at scale. arXiv preprint arXiv:1409.0798 (2014)

5. Bhattacherjee, S., Chavan, A., Huang, S., Deshpande, A., Parameswaran, A.G.: Principles of dataset versioning: exploring the recreation/storage tradeoff. CoRR abs/1505.05211 (2015). http://arxiv.org/abs/1505.05211

6. Blount, M., et al.: Real-time analysis for intensive care: development and deployment of the artemis analytic system. IEEE Eng. Med. Biol. Mag. **29**(2), 110–118 (2010). https://doi.org/10.1109/MEMB.2010.936454

7. Duarte, E., Gomes, D., Campos, D., Aguiar, R.L.: Distributed and scalable platform for collaborative analysis of massive time series data sets. In: Proceedings of the 8th International Conference on Data Science, Technology and Applications - Volume 1: DATA, pp. 41–52. INSTICC, SciTePress (2019). https://doi.org/10.5220/0007834700410052

8. Ellis, G., Dix, A.: A taxonomy of clutter reduction for information visualisation. IEEE Trans. Visual Comput. Graphics **13**(6), 1216–1223 (2007). https://doi.org/10.1109/TVCG.2007.70535

9. Eltabakh, M.Y., Aref, W.G., Elmagarmid, A.K., Ouzzani, M., Silva, Y.N.: Supporting annotations on relations. In: Proceedings of the 12th International Conference on Extending Database Technology: Advances in Database Technology, EDBT 2009, pp. 379–390. ACM, New York (2009). https://doi.org/10.1145/1516360.1516405, http://doi.acm.org/10.1145/1516360.1516405

10. Fielding, R.: Representational state transfer. In: Architectural Styles and the Design of Netowork-based Software Architecture, pp. 76–85 (2000)

11. Fowler, M.: Event sourcing. Online, Dec p. 18 (2005)

12. Freedman, M.: Timescaledb vs. influxdb: purpose built differently for time-series data (2019). https://blog.timescale.com/blog/timescaledb-vs-influxdb-for-time-series-data-timescale-influx-sql-nosql-36489299877/

13. Gilbert, S., Lynch, N.: Brewer's conjecture and the feasibility of consistent, available, partition-tolerant web services. SIGACT News **33**(2), 51–59 (2002). https://doi.org/10.1145/564585.564601, http://doi.acm.org/10.1145/564585.564601

14. Goldschmidt, T., Jansen, A., Koziolek, H., Doppelhamer, J., Breivold, H.P.: Scalability and robustness of time-series databases for cloud-native monitoring of industrial processes. In: 2014 IEEE 7th International Conference on Cloud Computing, pp. 602–609, June 2014. https://doi.org/10.1109/CLOUD.2014.86

15. Guyet, T., Garbay, C., Dojat, M.: Knowledge construction from time series data using a collaborative exploration system. J. Biomed. Inf. **40**(6), 672–687 (2007). https://doi.org/10.1016/j.jbi.2007.09.006, http://www.sciencedirect.com/science/article/pii/S1532046407001050, intelligent Data Analysis in Biomedicine

16. Hadavandi, E., Shavandi, H., Ghanbari, A.: Integration of genetic fuzzy systems and artificial neural networks for stock price forecasting. Knowl.-Based Syst. **23**(8), 800–808 (2010). https://doi.org/10.1016/j.knosys.2010.05.004, http://www.sciencedirect.com/science/article/pii/S0950705110000857

17. Hampton, L.: Eye or the tiger: benchmarking cassandra vs. timescaledb for time-series data (2018). https://blog.timescale.com/blog/time-series-data-cassandra-vs-timescaledb-postgresql-7c2cc50a89ce/
18. Harger, J.R., Crossno, P.J.: Comparison of open-source visual analytics toolkits, vol. 8294, pp. 8294–8294 - 10 (2012). https://doi.org/10.1117/12.911901, http://dx.doi.org/10.1117/12.911901
19. Healy, P.D., O'Reilly, R.D., Boylan, G.B., Morrison, J.P.: Web-based remote monitoring of live EEG. In: The 12th IEEE International Conference on e-Health Networking, Applications and Services, pp. 169–174, July 2010. https://doi.org/10.1109/HEALTH.2010.5556574
20. Healy, P.D., O'Reilly, R.D., Boylan, G.B., Morrison, J.P.: Interactive annotations to support collaborative analysis of streaming physiological data. In: 2011 24th International Symposium on Computer-Based Medical Systems (CBMS), pp. 1–5, June 2011. https://doi.org/10.1109/CBMS.2011.5999131
21. Huang, S., Xu, L., Liu, J., Elmore, A.J., Parameswaran, A.G.: Orpheusdb: bolt-on versioning for relational databases. PVLDB **10**(10), 1130–1141 (2017). http://www.vldb.org/pvldb/vol10/p1130-huang.pdf
22. Jensen, S.K., Pedersen, T.B., Thomsen, C.: Time series management systems: a survey. IEEE Trans. Knowl. Data Eng. **29**(11), 2581–2600 (2017). https://doi.org/10.1109/TKDE.2017.2740932
23. Kalakanti, A.K., Sudhakaran, V., Raveendran, V., Menon, N.: A comprehensive evaluation of NOSQL datastores in the context of historians and sensor data analysis. In: 2015 IEEE International Conference on Big Data (Big Data), pp. 1797–1806, October 2015. https://doi.org/10.1109/BigData.2015.7363952
24. Kalogeropoulos, D.A., Carson, E.R., Collinson, P.O.: Towards knowledge-based systems in clinical practice: Development of an integrated clinical information and knowledge management support system. Comput. Methods Programs Biomed. **72**(1), 65–80 (2003). https://doi.org/10.1016/S0169-2607(02)00118-9, http://www.sciencedirect.com/science/article/pii/S0169260702001189
25. Kamburugamuve, S., Wickramasinghe, P., Ekanayake, S., Wimalasena, C., Pathirage, M., Fox, G.C.: Tsmap3d: browser visualization of high dimensional time series data. In: 2016 IEEE International Conference on Big Data (Big Data), pp. 3583–3592 (2016)
26. Keraron, Y., Bernard, A., Bachimont, B.: Annotations to improve the using and the updating of digital technical publications. Res. Eng. Design **20**, 157–170 (2009)
27. Kiefer, R.: Timescaledb vs. postgresql for time-series: 20x higher inserts, 2000x faster deletes, 1.2x-14,000x faster queries (2017). https://blog.timescale.com/blog/timescaledb-vs-6a696248104e/
28. Kreps, J.: The log: what every software engineer should know about real-time data's unifying abstraction (2013). https://engineering.linkedin.com/distributed-systems/log-what-every-software-engineer-should-know-about-real-time-datas-unifying
29. Mathe, Z., Haen, C., Stagni, F.: Monitoring performance of a highly distributed and complex computing infrastructure in LHCB. In: Journal of Physics: Conference Series, vol. 898, p. 092028. IOP Publishing (2017)
30. Momjian, B.: Mvcc unmasked (2018). https://momjian.us/main/writings/pgsql/mvcc.pdf
31. O'Neil, P., Cheng, E., Gawlick, D., O'Neil, E.: The log-structured merge-tree (LSM-tree). Acta Informatica **33**(4), 351–385 (1996)
32. O'Reilly, R.D.: A distributed architecture for the monitoring and analysis of time series data (2015)
33. Pressly, Jr., W.B.S.: TSPAD: a tablet-pc based application for annotation and collaboration on time series data. In: Proceedings of the 46th Annual Southeast Regional Conference on XX, ACM-SE 46, pp. 527–528. ACM, New York (2008). https://doi.org/10.1145/1593105.1593249, http://doi.acm.org/10.1145/1593105.1593249

34. Provos, N., Mazieres, D.: A future-adaptable password scheme (1999)
35. Pungilă, C., Fortiş, T.F., Aritoni, O.: Benchmarking database systems for the requirements of sensor readings. IETE Tech. Rev. **26**(5), 342–349 (2009). https://doi.org/10.4103/0256-4602.55279, http://www.tandfonline.com/doi/abs/10.4103/0256-4602.55279
36. van Renesse, R., Schneider, F.B.: Chain replication for supporting high throughput and availability. In: Proceedings of the 6th Conference on Symposium on Operating Systems Design & Implementation - Volume 6, OSDI 2004, p.7. USENIX Association, Berkeley(2004). http://dl.acm.org/citation.cfm?id=1251254.1251261
37. Snodgrass, R.T.: Temporal databases. In: Frank, A.U., Campari, I., Formentini, U. (eds.) GIS 1992. LNCS, vol. 639, pp. 22–64. Springer, Heidelberg (1992). https://doi.org/10.1007/3-540-55966-3_2
38. Sow, D., Biem, A., Blount, M., Ebling, M., Verscheure, O.: Body sensor data processing using stream computing. In: Proceedings of the International Conference on Multimedia Information Retrieval, MIR 2010, pp. 449–458, ACM, New York (2010). https://doi.org/10.1145/1743384.1743465, http://doi.acm.org/10.1145/1743384.1743465

Optimizing Steering of Roaming Traffic with A-number Billing Under a Rolling Horizon Policy

Ahmet Şahin$^{(\boxtimes)}$ [ID], Kenan Cem Demirel [ID], Ege Ceyhan [ID], and Erinc Albey [ID]

Department of Industrial Engineering, Özyeğin University, 34794 Istanbul, Turkey
{ahmet.sahin,cem.demirel,ege.ceyhan}@ozu.edu.tr,
erinc.albey@ozyegin.edu.tr

Abstract. In this study, we focus on single service steering international roaming traffic (SIRT) problem by considering telecommunication operators' agreements and "a-number billing" while keeping service quality above a certain threshold. The steering decision is made considering the origin and destination of the call, total volume requirement of bilateral agreements, quality threshold and price quote of partner operators. We develop an optimization model that considers these requirements while satisfying projected demand requirements. We suggest a framework based on rolling horizon mechanism for demand forecasting and policy updating. The results show that the steering cost is decreased approximately 11% with deterministic demand and 10% with forecasted demand compared to the base cost value provided by the company. Also, the model provides approximately 26% decrease in unsatisfied committed volume in agreements.

Keywords: Steering international roaming traffic · A-number billing · Linear programming · Demand forecasting · Rolling horizon

1 Introduction

Like in many other markets, increasing number of service providers has escalated the competition in the telecommunication sector. The high number of potential partner operators, who can provide steering of roaming, decreased traffic movement charges, hence the profit margins of the operators have decreased. Making the right cross connection agreements for minimized international traffic steering costs became more crucial and complicated for the operators which are trying to survive in this competitive sector.

Due to the instantly changing market positions, steering decisions should be updated rapidly to increase profits and decrease total traffic steering cost. In most of the companies, steering decisions are given manually. Almost daily changing price quotes and excessive number of possible steering options makes it impossible to find the optimal decisions manually.

© Springer Nature Switzerland AG 2020
S. Hammoudi et al. (Eds.): DATA 2019, CCIS 1255, pp. 83–95, 2020.
https://doi.org/10.1007/978-3-030-54595-6_5

Telecommunication network design related optimization models are the frequently studied problems in the telecommunication sector related literature [13]. Studies on telecommunication network designing and optimization for demand dependent situations are very common [4,6,14], while optimization model for service management is not frequently studied.

Mixed-integer linear formulations are observed under the steering international roaming traffic (SIRT) type of problem with distinct agreement methods in [12]. The objective is to decide the quantity of voice traffic that will be steered to optimize the wholesales margin that occurs, when steering some voice traffic to different operators from different countries.

A mixed-integer linear formulation is provided for SIRT with multi-service property in [3]. Objective of the model is to minimize the sum of the wholesale roaming costs linked to the commercial agreements. These agreements are between Orange Telecommunications Groups (OTG) and operators in North America and Europe, which constitutes 43 partner operators in total. The model is run for five simulated instances based on the yearly forecasts of the amount of roaming traffics of OTG subscribers in each visited country and the problem is solved simultaneously for data and voice traffics with different agreement types. Four out of five instances' optimal results are computed in less than five minutes. A feasible solution for the fifth problem is also found but with optimality gap of 0.21%. It is assumed that whole roaming traffic is distributed randomly and evenly to the partner operators in the corresponding countries. The provided optimization model brings 30% improvement in the OTG's wholesale roaming cost.

One important missing aspect in these studies is that none of them considers quality thresholds for steered calls. According to [11], in a market where traffic steerings are perfectly performed, no operator has market power and the competitive advantage is always in the side of lower prices. For this reason, quality is a necessity rather than being an important criterion for operators who are advantageous in terms of their market positions to maintain these advantages. In [15], SIRT problem is considered with single service that concerns a telecommunication's operators' agreements with other operators in order to enable subscribers access services, without interruption, when they are out of operators coverage area. An optimization model considering agreement constraints and quality requirements, while satisfying subscribers demand over a predetermined time interval is proposed.

In this paper, various extensions to [15] are proposed. First, the problem formulation along with the considered data set is extended such that more realistic scenarios will be solvable. Moreover, a demand prediction module is developed and results of the module for outgoing calls is integrated into the optimization model. More specifically, a new steering model for single service (voice steering by oneself) with quality of call with pending "a-number billing" is included under a dataset of call steering with forecasted demand belonging to a real-life case is proposed. Turkish GSM sector leader, Turkcell, has provided the dataset. Roughly 10% decrease in cost of steering is achieved by automating and optimizing steering decisions. For hte stochastic outgoing demand, a rolling horizon approach is applied and forecasts are made for certain intervals to reflect the predicted demands into the model. For the model's output; percentage ratio are computed for each prefix, origin and carrier basis. A real test data set is used (which is hidden from the forecast model) to estimate the actual cost of steering decisions.

The rest of the paper is organized as follows: The problem is described and the data is introduced in Sect. 2. The steering model with call quality considering "a-number billing" is described in Sect. 3. Results are presented in Sect. 4 and the conclusion is provided in Sect. 5.

2   Problem Description

Operators' roaming services in telecommunication sector can be classified in two different markets, which are retail markets and wholesale markets [16]. Retail market's roaming service is for selling service to own users while wholesale market's roaming service is letting other operator's customers in different countries use network, when they are not in their origin country. Other operators are called "partner operators". If there is no chance to successfully provide end-to-end call with using single operator's network, then the operator interconnects with other operator (Fig. 1), that is in order to satisfy customer demand, traffic is steered to the partner operator. Different cases can be realized for steering operations.

A call started from an operator may end at another operator's network. In more complex scenarios, a call starts at operator (originate), then continues at another operator and then ends in another operator (destination). In chain steering cases like this, every member of the chain should have multiple interconnect agreement between neighbour members. Agreements shall be managed by operators for cost reduction and efficient use of networks. Operators should manage these agreements in order to use their networks efficiently, reduce costs, and increase margins.

As the European Parliament's new regulation about telecommunication operator steering, which is accepted in 2017, different tariffs can be applied according to call's origin which are in the same destination group by using "a-number" information. For the sake of the operators, they started to get avoided from abuses based on permanent or residence related to an European Union country. Operators are avoided from irregular circumstances in the domestic market. Different tariffs are applied from the different origins with the same destinations. Thus, tariffs are decided by country codes or route of origination. Before this regulation is executed, B-number rating, billing and routing was being concerned by carriers. A need occurred on changing schemes and focusing on both billing type which are origin (A-number) and destination (B-number).

The problem we aim to solve in this paper is to steer the international voice traffic of the home operator, Turkcell, with minimum cost and keep the quality on acceptable level by considering the origin of the call. International call steering consists of two parts: 1) outgoing traffic steering, 2) incoming traffic steering.

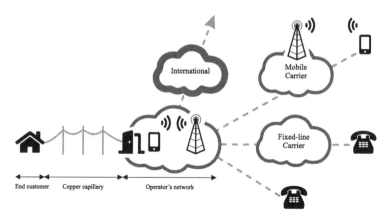

Fig. 1. Network diagram of the home operator [15].

On daily basis, outgoing traffic states the steered volume to partner operators. Home operators and partner operators have special agreements for traffic steering which are also called commitment agreements. While increasing the business volume, agreements may not point to a profit at an ongoing period. Agreements may also lead to price discounts or commercial trust in upcoming periods. Additionally, the quality aspect is leading these agreements to becomes more important on behalf of customer satisfaction. Keeping the quality on a sufficient grade at the outgoing steering decisions is crucial as the cost of the steering.

Incoming traffic steering lies outside from the focus of this study since it described in detail at [15].

2.1 Dataset

In this part, data acquisition for the inputs of the model and the properties of data are described. The objective of the model is to keep the quality level above a particular threshold level, while decreasing the traffic steering cost. In order to create the model, the following data is used:

- Unit price per minute based on origin (A-number) and destination (B-number) (Tariff)
- Locations where operators provide service
- Outgoing demand information
- Details of agreements with other operators
- Call Detail Record (to determine quality metric)

Turkcell is the market leader in the Turkish GSM market with 44% market share and the annual income of US\$4.4B in 2018 [17]. In addition to the 33.8 million customers in the Turkish market, Turkcell is a global company and it serves 12.2 million customers in Azerbaijan, Kazakhstan, Georgia, Moldova,

Northern Cyprus, and Ukraine. Turkcell has international roaming agreements with 622 operators in 201 countries as of 2018.

Call Detail Record (CDR) is a detailed dataset containing the time of call, length, competition status, source phone number, and destination phone number. In this work, CDR data is available for international traffic between 01.03.2019-30.03.2019 in worldwide. Prefixes in the CDR dataset that daily occurred steering process in one month is included in works in order to obtain meaningful forecasts. In the outgoing traffic, there are 153 operators and 2364 prefixes in the data. Also, the information about agreements of 24 operators and 279 locations are available in the data.

When the distributions of demands coming from designated areas and goes to a specific prefix, generally two characteristics is observed. Some of the demands are clearly containing seasonality, while some of them are in the wavy structure and free from the season. Examples from these two characteristics can be seen in Fig. 2a and Fig. 2b. The figures show the demand for the calls on a one-month period.

In order to test a more realistic scenario in which the decisions are made one week earlier than the actual demand realization, 1 step and 2 step forecasts are calculated by applying the rolling horizon approach using weekly, two weekly, and three weekly data.

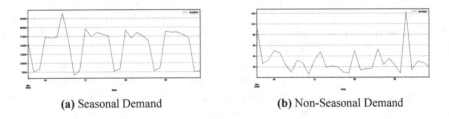

(a) Seasonal Demand   (b) Non-Seasonal Demand

Fig. 2. Characteristics of demand.

2.2   Demand Forecasting

We choose to utilize time series models in order to predict future demand values. Among many others, two commonly used linear time series models in the literature are Moving Average (MA) and Autoregressive (AR) models. A combination of AR and MA models, namely, Autoregressive Moving Average (ARMA) and Autoregressive Integrated Moving Average (ARIMA) models are also very frequently studied in the literature. ARIMA model can be used when the data is non-seasonal and non-stationary [2]. A different type of ARIMA, named Seasonal Autoregressive Integrated Moving Average (SARIMA), model is also proposed as a seasonal time series forecasting model [1,2,8,9]. To work with a data set with seasonal components, Box and Jenkins [1] have proposed SARIMA and in order to eliminate non-stationary structure from the time series, seasonal differencing of appropriate order is used.

In this study, ARIMA and SARIMA models are used. After splitting the data to train and test set, we used grid search for searching parameters for ARIMA and SARIMA. For scoring and selecting the best model, the Akaike Information Criterion (AIC) scoring method is used. The method can be shown to have a basis in frequentist-based inference and information theory. To use AIC for model selection, we simply choose the model giving the smallest AIC over the set of models considered [5]. For the test set, the forecast is done with selected parameters and an appropriate model. Then, the mathematical model is fed with the corresponding forecast.

2.3 Agreements

International roaming traffic increments caused the competitive wholesale roaming sector to be reshaped. To offer better commercial solutions in the reshaped sector, trade agreements are matured and named as International Roaming Agreement (IRA). Home operators established unilateral unit prices named International Operator Tariffs (IoT). In the bilateral agreements, the large traffic volumes can push the unit prices to lower levels. Mutual commitments are the basis of these agreements.

There are four basic IRA's used in the wholesale roaming market: Quantity (QNT), Incremental (INC), Balanced/Unbalanced (BUB), and Send-or-Pay (SOP). The pricing schema of these models are given in Fig. 3. The detailed description of these models can be found in [3].

Turkcell is one of the prescriptive operators in the European region. Turkcell is using a distinguished pricing method, which is very much alike to the BUB model. However, in this specified pricing method, exceeding the volume of the commitments is paid by negotiating according to the fulfillment rates of both parties. In this method, the final cost is determined by negotiations based on business relationships. With accurate demand forecasts and minimization of the steering costs, Turkcell takes advantage in the negotiation phase.

The problem has two types of partner operators, which are committed operator (CO) and uncommitted operators (UO). There is no assurance on the service volume and tariff is priced on a minutely basis at UO. Better price on a predetermined volume of calling minutes offer is the leading sense of the agreements.

Committed operators commonly establish how the termination service will be exchanged. Compensation occurs between parties which send more and others for the amount of traffic surplus basis. For settlement purposes inter-network traffic measurements are compulsory for this fact.

In the scope of these agreements, operators agree to steer their traffic to each other in certain time intervals and particular volumes. These agreements haven't got any legal bindings but on behalf of business relations, both operators try to obey the rule of lower limits at agreements. Agreements are described in detail at [15].

The example of agreement with a CO is shown in Table 1.

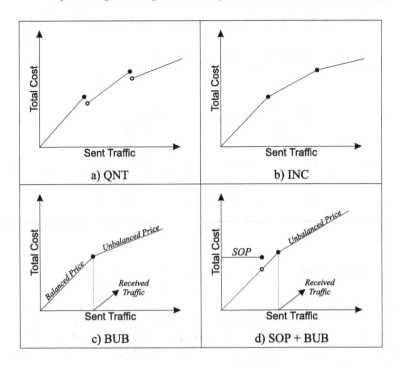

Fig. 3. Payment models [3].

2.4   Analysis of Quality Metrics

There are four main quality metrics that are computed with CDR data and recommended by the International Telecommunication Union. These four metrics are Answer Seizure Ratio (ASR), Network Efficiency Ratio (NER), Average Call Duration (ACD), and Post Dial Delay (PDD) [10]. These metrics are observed in detail at previous study and concluded as using NER is more appropriate since it is more comprehensive and NER can determine threshold better while measuring network quality [15].

Measuring the capability of network calling the terminal is called Network Efficiency Ratio (NER). NER excluded customer and terminal behaviors when compared with ASR. Network Efficiency Ratio speaks better for pure network performance.

$$NER = \frac{\text{Seizures resulting in Answer message or User Failure}}{\text{Total seizures}} \tag{1}$$

Table 1. Example of agreements with CO [15].

Committed operator	Currency		
X	EUR		
Start date	End date		
1.07.2017	31.12.2017		
Outgoing traffic		Incoming traffic	
Location	Volume	Location	Volume
D1	8,500,000	D5	20,000,000
D2	1,000,000	D6	7,500,000
D3	2,250,000	D7	10,000,000
D4	1,500,000		

3 A-number Steering Model with Call Quality

After data analysis and processing, a mathematical model for steering of international roaming is proposed with a cost minimization objective. The model determines steering decisions for international roaming traffic to each operator, destination (B-number), and origin (A-number) while keeping the quality on an acceptable level.

The notation used in the mathematical model; sets, parameters, decision variables, and the proposed mathematical model are provided below:

Sets:

- i = operator,
- j = destination prefix,
- k = destination location,
- z = origin prefix,
- P_{ij}^z = possible operator, destination prefix and origin prefix matches,
- G_{jk}^z = prefix and location matches,
- A_{ik} = operator and location matches in agreements.

Parameters:

- d_j^z = Outgoing voice demand from origin prefix z to destination prefix j,
- c_{ij}^z = Unit cost of outgoing voice traffic from origin prefix z to destination prefix j over operator i,
- V_{ik} = Volume of agreement for location k with operator i,
- q_{ij} = Network Efficiency Ratio (NER) of operator i for destination prefix j,
- q_t = Quality threshold,
- M = Big Number.

Decision Variables:

- x_{ij}^z = amount of voice steering to prefix j over operator i,
- u_{ik}^+ = amount of missing voice steering to location k over operator i,

LP Model:

$$\min \quad \sum_i \sum_j c_{ij}^z x_{ij}^z + \sum_i \sum_k M u_{ik}^+ \tag{2}$$

$$s.t. \quad \sum_{i \in P_{ij}^z} x_{ij}^z = d_j^z \qquad \forall j, z \tag{3}$$

$$\sum_{i \in P_{ij}} q_{ij} x_{ij}^z \geq q_t \sum_{i \in P_{ij}} x_{ij}^z \qquad \forall j, z \tag{4}$$

$$\sum_{j \in G_{jk}} x_{ij}^z + u_{ik}^+ \geq V_{ik} \qquad \forall i, k \in A_{ik} \tag{5}$$

$$x_{ij}^z \geq 0 \quad \forall i, j \tag{6}$$

$$u_{ik}^+ \geq 0 \quad \forall i, j \tag{7}$$

The Linear Programming (LP) model presented in Eqs. (2) through (7) aims to minimize the total steering cost and penalizes the unsatisfied agreements' volume. In the objective function (Eq. 2), Big M is a sufficiently large number that aims to firstly minimize u_{ik}^+ values (set the smallest positive values possible).

Constraint 3 ensures that the outgoing demand is met for each prefix. Constraint 4 guarantees that if steering occurs from origin prefix z to destination prefix j over operator i, the average quality of steering has to be greater than the quality threshold. Constraint 5 ensures that it satisfies the deal volume for each operator and each location. The rest of the constraints (Constraint 6 and 7) are non-negativity constraints for variables.

We implement the model by using Python 3.7 and GUROBI Solver [7] for LP. We perform all experiments on an Intel Core i7-8550U 1.8 GHz machine with 16 GB RAM.

The next section presents the scenarios we test and discussion of the findings.

4   Results

Data is applicable for international outgoing traffic. The interval of the data is 01.03.2019–30.03.2019 globally as mentioned before. The problem has definite assumptions. Firstly, the following assumptions are made for estimating the quality of the operators when historic quality data of the operators is not available: 1)If a given prefix's average quality is missing, then, the location average is used for the corresponding operator. 2) If the operator has no information about the location at all, all location's quality average is used. Secondly, steering costs are calculated based on the same exchange rate.

Results are computed under 3 different scenarios. In all 3 scenarios, the quality threshold is determined as Turkcell's historic quality average which is 78.72% and the first 10 days' data is kept for the training of the forecast model. In the first scenario, no forecast is applied and deterministic demands are directly processed in the model for 11th to 30th days. The model developed for this scenario represents the real-life scenario. In the second scenario, first, 10 days' demands are used to forecast 11th to 30th days' demands. In the third and last scenario, the rolling horizon approach is used and by using the first 10 days' data from 11th to 20th days data is forecasted while using the first 20 days' data for forecasting 21st to 30th days' data. Benchmark between results of scenarios in this study and Turkcell's independent (not using any model of this study) results are presented on Table 2.

Table 2. Total costs and Average quality rates.

	Total cost ($)	q_a (%)
Base	5,584,203.29	78.72
Scenario 1	4,912,877.89	82.23
Scenario 2	5,028,232.28	79.98
Scenario 3	4,944,826.17	81.18

Table 3. Sum of unsatisfied commitment minutes.

	$\sum_{ik} u_{ik}^+$ (min)
Base	597,831
Scenario 1	307,279
Scenario 2	384,534
Scenario 3	344,982

According to Table 2, 12.1% cost reduction is provided using a deterministic scenario in which the demand is known exactly. In the second scenario, the model resulted in 10.0% improvement containing forecast errors. In the third and last scenario improvement is increased to 11.5% containing forecast errors. The reason for this improvement is the rolling horizon approach converges to reality. In Table 3, the mentioned forecast errors can be observed for a chosen prefix.

According to Table 3, the first 10 days' forecasts look appropriate to real life, but forecasts after that converge to average demand, and the total error increases. In Graph B and C, the rolling horizon approach is presented. Demand forecasts for 11th to 20th and 21st to 30th days look similar to the real demands.

In another example, the real demands of the last 20 days for the chosen prefix are 215K min while in the second scenario forecast is 240K min and in the third

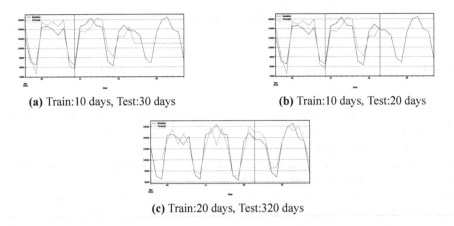

(a) Train:10 days, Test:30 days   (b) Train:10 days, Test:20 days

(c) Train:20 days, Test:320 days

Fig. 4. Train:10 days, Test:30 days

scenario forecast is 259K min. So forecast error is −5% in the first scenario while 3% in the second scenario for the corresponding prefix. The fact worthy of notice is when the forecasted demand is smaller than the actual demand, in order to fill up the agreement quotes, the developed model tries to steer calls mostly to the committed operators. In the case of high demands, since the agreement quotes will be fulfilled, the model can act more flexible in the steering decision and provides cost-benefit (Fig. 4).

When we observe all prefix's demand forecasts, the first scenario's average forecast error is 28.8%, while in the rolling horizon approach's average forecast error is 21.4%.

5 Conclusion

Operator agreements are made between contracted operators in order to decrease their service costs by steering the calls if the destination of the call is out of the operator's coverage area. The steering decision is based on the destination of the call, the price quote of the partner operator for that location, and the service quality threshold of the partner operator. Besides, according to the new law adopted by the European Commission in 2017, "a-number" which indicates the origin of the call, is also a factor for pricing. Finding the optimal steering decision under the agreement conditions and other company-specific requests is called the steering international roaming traffic (SIRT) problem.

We propose a solution to the SIRT problem with a single service by developing an optimization model that takes into account agreement constraints, a-number billing, and a quality threshold while meeting subscribers' demand over a predetermined period. Incoming steering demands are used under three different scenarios: a) deterministic demand, b) 20-day demand forecasting, generated by using 10-day data, c) the rolling horizon approach. In the rolling horizon approach, the train data set of the forecasting model is expanded and the forecasting accuracy is improved.

The results show that the steering cost is reduced, on the average, approximately 11% although the quality of the steered calls is kept above the base quality level.

As a future step, a simulation-based decision support system may be developed to monitor how to set commitment values of future agreements under different scenarios. The developed model may also be tested with other agreement models provided in the literature. In addition, the common decisions of home operators under certain conditions could be included in the model yielding a more complex mixed-integer programming model. Assuming solving large size instances in reasonable time may not be possible, developing time-efficient heuristic algorithms will be an imminent future research direction.

References

1. Box, G.E., Jenkins, G.M., Reinsel, G.: Time Series Analysis: Forecasting and Control. Holden-Day, San Francisco (1970)
2. Brockwell, P.J., Davis, R.A.: Introduction to Time Series and Forecasting. STS. Springer, Cham (2016). https://doi.org/10.1007/978-3-319-29854-2
3. Esteves, J.J.A., Boulmier, G., Chardy, M., Bechler, A.: Optimization of the steering of the international multi-services roaming traffic. In: 2018 IEEE 29th Annual International Symposium on Personal, Indoor and Mobile Radio Communications (PIMRC), pp. 246–252. IEEE (2018)
4. Flippo, O.E., Kolen, A.W., Koster, A.M., van de Leensel, R.L.: A dynamic programming algorithm for the local access telecommunication network expansion problem. Eur. J. Oper. Res. **127**(1), 189–202 (2000)
5. Friedman, J., Hastie, T., Tibshirani, R.: The Elements of Statistical Learning. Springer Series in Statistics, vol. 10. Springer, New York (2001). https://doi.org/10.1007/978-0-387-21606-5
6. Gendreau, M., Potvin, J.Y., Smires, A., Soriano, P.: Multi-period capacity expansion for a local access telecommunications network. Eur. J. Oper. Res. **172**(3), 1051–1066 (2006)
7. Gurobi Optimization, LLC: Gurobi optimizer reference manual (2019). http://www.gurobi.com
8. Hipel, K.W., McLeod, A.I.: Time Series Modelling of Water Resources and Environmental Systems, vol. 45. Elsevier, Amsterdam (1994)
9. Hyndman, R.J., Athanasopoulos, G.: Forecasting: Principles and Practice. OTexts, Melbourne (2018)
10. ITU-T: E. 425 internal automatic observations. ITU-T Recommendation (2002)
11. Lacasa, J.D.: Competition for partners: strategic games in wholesale international roaming. In: European Regional Conference of the International Telecommunications Society. ITS, Budapest (2011)
12. Martins, C.L., da Conceição Fonseca, M., Pato, M.V.: Modeling the steering of international roaming traffic. Eur. J. Oper. Res. **261**(2), 735–754 (2017)
13. Pióro, M., Medhi, D.: Routing, Flow, and Capacity Design in Communication and Computer Networks. Elsevier, Amsterdam (2004)

14. Riis, M., Andersen, K.A.: Multiperiod capacity expansion of a telecommunications connection with uncertain demand. Comput. Oper. Res. **31**(9), 1427–1436 (2004)
15. Sahin, A., Demirel, K.C., Albey, E., Gürsun, G.: International roaming traffic optimization with call quality. In: Hammoudi, S., Quix, C., Bernardino, J. (eds.) Proceedings of the 8th International Conference on Data Science, Technology and Applications, DATA 2019, Prague, Czech Republic, 26–28 July 2019, pp. 92–99. SciTePress (2019)
16. Salsas, R., Koboldt, C.: Roaming free?: roaming network selection and inter-operator tariffs. Inf. Econ. Policy **16**(4), 497–517 (2004)
17. Turkcell: Turkcell annual report 2018 (2018). https://s.turkcell.com.tr/hakkimizda/en/yatirimciiliskileri/InvestorReportLibrary/Turkcell-AR-2018-ENG.pdf/

A Web-Based Decision Support System for Quality Prediction in Manufacturing Using Ensemble of Regressor Chains

Kenan Cem Demirel[ID], Ahmet Şahin[(✉)][ID], and Erinc Albey[ID]

Department of Industrial Engineering, Özyeğin University, 34794 Istanbul, Turkey
{cem.demirel,ahmet.sahin}@ozu.edu.tr
erinc.albey@ozyegin.edu.tr

Abstract. In this study we construct a decision support system (DSS), which utilizes the production process parameters to predict the quality characteristics of final products in two different manufacturing plants. Using the idea of regressor chains, an ensemble method is developed to attain the highest prediction accuracy. Collected data is divided into two sets, namely "normal" and "unusual", using local outlier factor method. The prediction performance is tested separately for each set. It is seen that the ensemble idea shows its competence especially in situations, where collected data is classified as "unusual". We tested the proposed method in two different real-life cases: textile manufacturing process and plastic injection molding process. Proposed DSS supports online decisions through live process monitoring screens and provides real time quality predictions, which help to minimize the total number of nonconforming products.

Keywords: Industry 4.0 · Quality prediction · Ensemble methods · Regressor chains · Decision support system.

1 Introduction

Data-based process analysis becomes easier with the advances in data collection and processing systems, that are specifically developed for industrial plants. With the Industrial internet-of-things (IIoT) revolution, the concept of fog computing is changing the way data is being treated in manufacturing plants. Increasing ease of applicability (in terms of both budget and deployment/installation wise) of the platforms, which enable i) high-resolution live data collection and ii) processing advance analytic tasks instantly, make the deployment of live quality prediction and predictive maintenance models way easier now, hence more common, compared to past decade. Developed data-driven prediction models can be used to i) improve analytic processes and ii) assist operational and tactical decisions need to be taken during the production. Decision support systems (DSS) specifically designed to operate in these modern

© Springer Nature Switzerland AG 2020
S. Hammoudi et al. (Eds.): DATA 2019, CCIS 1255, pp. 96–114, 2020.
https://doi.org/10.1007/978-3-030-54595-6_6

platforms and capable to host these complex models become a necessity in order to run the production processes in a smooth and error free manner. These DSS solutions can be developed locally as separate software for production facilities and related prodcution lines; or they can be developed as web-based system to cover all production facilities and their sub-units.

In this paper, a web-based DSS is developed, which aims to inform operators about quality problems that may come up during the live production. The DSS developed in this work contains a web-based front-end graphical user interface (GUI) that is designed according the user needs; a database to keep user information, user inputs, live production data, production logs, quality reports and predictive models, and a predictive model layer (see Fig. 6, in Sect. 3.5). The web-based system assists the end-user to access the data of selected production lines and facilities and create reports on-line.

DSS we developed is customized to satisfy the needs of quality prediction applications in two distinct industrial plants (with two different processes): a textile manufacturing process and a sub assembly part (rear cover) production process for white goods industry. For the predictive model layer, we first implement a single target predictive model by using Random Forest Regression, which is shown to be superior in our previous study [14]. In [14], the performance of the proposed approach is tested using three different quality metrics. Considering the performance of single target models, we propose an ensemble algorithm, which is based on regressor chain idea. The paper's most important finding is that once production becomes different from the usual conditions, for some performance metrics, prediction accuracy of the single target models falls dramatically. The ensemble of regressor chains idea is useful for such cases, resulting in a lower prediction error in two-thirds of the dataset. In addition, the developed meta-learner is embedded into the developed DSS system, which is customized for quality prediction in production facilities. With the development of a prediction engine that provides live quality predictions and provides recommendations for ideal production parameters, developed DSS is launched as the first live-in-industry 4.0 application of both plants.

The rest of the paper is organized as follows: Sect. 2 provides brief background information on the textile and rear cover manufacturing processes and outlines the methodology used in the study. In Sect. 3, the proposed solution methodology is presented along with DSS details and description of the prediction process. Section 4 presents the results of the numerical analysis, which is followed by the concluding remarks.

2   Background and Methodology

In this section, we present background information regarding the two manufacturing processes considered in this paper, namely textile manufacturing and an injection molding process on rear cover manufacturing for white good appliances. In addition, we present the general idea about the methodology of choice in building the predictive model and proposed DSS.

2.1 Textile Manufacturing Processes

Textile production consists of three main stages: 1) warping, 2) weaving, 3) finishing.

In the first step, winding, unraveling, sizing, weaving draft and knotting processes are performed and the yarns are made suitable for weaving. The yarns are wound up in the desired tension and arrangement, thereby imparting strength into the yarns.

After warping, the fabrics are processed such as mouth opening, weft insertion and tufting to ensure that the warp and weft yarns intersect.

In the finishing stage, which is the last stage of production, the desired color, touch and special effects are provided to the fabric. After the last stage is completed, random samples are taken from the produced yarns and sent to the laboratory for quality control tests. The laboratory performs quality tests for each sample and prepares a quality report.

In this work, we only consider the finishing stage, hence data collection, modelling and development of DSS covers solely the finishing phase of the selected textile manufacturing process.

2.2 Rear Cover Manufacturing Processes

Rear cover manufacturing by injection molding processes consists of six main stages: 1) drying, 2) plasticization, 3) closure of mold, 4) injection, 5) cooling, 6) disposal.

In the first stage, the raw material is kept in the drying unit for a sufficient period depending on the properties of the raw material to be used in the process.

In the plasticization, the lid of the dried raw material feeder is opened and pushed to the heating units with the help of worm screw. Here, melting material passes through the heaters of different temperatures and moves towards the injector nozzle. The temperatures of the heaters are determined by taking into consideration the factors such as melting temperature, fluidity value, wall thickness of the raw material to be used.

After that, the movement of the worm screw ceases and sufficient material remains in the injecting nozzle. One important thing to note here is that the amount of material injected into the mold should be the same for each time to get material of the same quality and weight.

Before starting the injection, the two halves of the mold are securely closed by the clamping unit. Both halves of the mold are joined to the injection unit, while one of the molds is movable in the axial direction. The hydraulic unit brings the vise molds together and the injection process is started.

In the injection stage, the plastic raw material in the form of small particles reaches the molds through the feeder and then through the end of the nozzle with the help of worm screws. Due to the complexity and variation of the fluidity of the plastic material in the molten state, it is difficult to determine the exact injection time [11].

Once injected, the plastic material begins to cool down. As a result of the cooling stage, the plastic material begins to solidify by taking the shape of the mold into which it is injected. The mold cannot be opened during the required cooling stage. Cooling time can be calculated according to the wall thickness, thermodynamic and mechanical properties of various plastic materials.

Once the cooling period is over, the material cools and solidifies in the mold. Then, it is expelled from the mold by injection ram. The pusher is placed in one half of the mold, and when the mold is opened, the pusher shaft moves forward and actuates the pins. Once the part has been ejected from the mold, the molds are reassembled by the vice unit and prepared for the next injection process.

Within the scope of this paper, we are going to study predicting linearity, flatness, and density which are three important quality metrics for the final product that is produced through the injection molding process, by considering process signals such as injection pressure, resistance heating, clamping motor vibration, etc.

2.3   Ensemble of Regressor Chains

In this paper, we are going to focus on a real-life application of the Ensemble of Regressor Chains (ERC) proposed in [15], which is an extension of the Regressor Chain (RC) approach.

The main idea behind the RC is chaining single-target regressors sequentially in random order. In the RC, selected subsets of the target variables are added to the training set independently and predictive models are trained for each subset in the chain order. After the training phase, the first target variable in the chain is predicted by the first model, and predicted target values are added to the test set as a new input vector for prediction of the next target variable. The same process is repeated for all subsequent targets in the chain. RC approach has been explained thoroughly in our previous work [14]. Graphical illustration of RC is shown in Fig. 1.

Because different sequences in RC cause significantly different predictive performances, the Ensemble of Regressor Chains (ERC) method is proposed by [15]. In the ERC, predictions are made by using all permutations of chain sequences, and the mean of the predicted values for each target variable is provided as the final prediction of that target variable. However, it is possible to apply the ERC method that considers all possible sequences only when the number of target variables is relatively small.

We choose Random Forest Regressor (RFR) as the learner of the ERC meta-learner, due to its superior performance compared to other regressors when ERC method is of concern, [14]. Random Forest is an ensemble learning method that aims to improve predictive accuracy and prevent over-fitting by fitting multiple decision trees on various sub-samples of the dataset and combining them under a single meta-estimator [3].

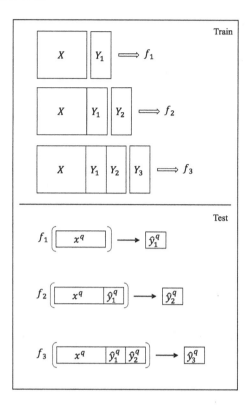

Fig. 1. Graphical illustration of RC [14].

2.4   Decision Support System

This study presents a model-driven decision support system (DSS) that produces predictions for quality metrics by using a web-based platform. A model-driven DSS is described as a system that uses algebraic, decision-analytic, optimization, or simulation models to support decisions [13]. In general, models in a model-driven DSS represent a simplified version of the reality [6]. Decision analysis models are used for statistical tools and methods such as decision tree analysis [12], multi-criteria decision analysis [8], and probability forecasting [9]. Decision support systems have an important use in the area of production management, operations management, and supply chain management [2,10]. Model-driven DSS is designed to configure system and model parameters for analyzing a given situation by the user to enhance the decision-making process. The main component of the system is one or more models that provide functionality in a model-driven DSS architecture. In general, optimization models and simulation techniques are used to make decisions. However, today, with the recent studies of machine learning, predictive models have also been used as the model base.

3   Experimental Setup

3.1   Datasets

In this study, we consider two different datasets obtained from paired process data (signals) of textile manufacturing and rear cover manufacturing of a white good appliance. The textile dataset is also used in [14].

In the first dataset, namely the textile dataset, there are total of 1,511 rows, one row for each lab sample, and each lab sample has 19 signal values, such that weaving speed, temperature, and yarn tension. Each row in the dataset also contains three quality metrics to be predicted: water permeability (Metric 1), tear strength (Metric 2), and abrasion resistance (Metric 3), which are obtained after lab sample assessed in the laboratory.

The statistical summary (the sample mean value, standard deviation, coefficient of variation, minimum, and the maximum values) of all 19 features is shown in Table 1. Also, the Z-normalization results of target metrics 1, 2 and 3 are given in Fig. 2. After examining the target data, it is observed that the variance of Z-values of tear strength is much higher than that of other metrics.

Table 1. Feature summary statistics of the textile dataset [14].

Feature	Mean	Std	CoV^3	Min	Max
0	70.0	1.0	0.0	65.7	74.5
1	−10.8	1.2	−0.1	−14.5	−7.7
2	−4.2	1.2	−0.3	−8.5	−2.2
3	−0.2	0.1	−0.3	−0.4	0.0
4	−0.3	0.2	−0.5	−0.3	0.0
5	7.4	2.1	0.3	0.0	14.8
6	31.9	2.6	0.1	28.5	53.7
7	302.9	77.1	0.3	198.9	401.4
8	27.2	0.0	0.0	27.2	27.2
9	37.9	0.0	0.0	37.9	37.9
10	25.2	2.8	0.1	20.3	31.8
11	49.9	4.1	0.1	42.3	57.3
12	63.0	6.9	0.1	44.4	70.4
13	28.3	1.6	0.1	23.2	32.3
14	25.3	2.2	0.1	18.8	31.8
15	152.6	4.9	0.0	143.4	163.7
16	146.5	8.8	0.1	119.1	154.6
17	225.8	0.6	0.0	225.1	226.3
18	20.7	1.5	0.1	17.7	25.2

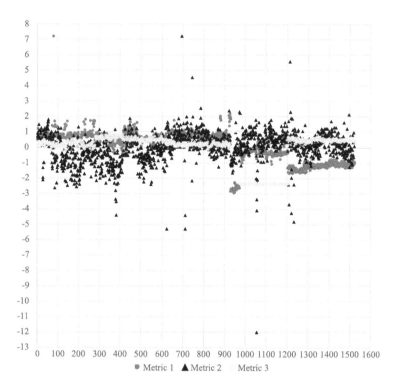

Fig. 2. Z-normalization scores of the textile dataset target variables [14].

In the second dataset, namely the plastic dataset, there are a total of 428 rows, one row for each laboratory sample. Each laboratory sample has 46 signal values, such as injection and nozzle pressure, resistance heating signal, clamping motor vibration and hopper temperature as algorithm inputs; and three quality metrics, linearity (Metric 1), flatness (Metric 2), and density (Metric 3).

The statistical summary of the feature set for plastic dataset is listed in Table 2. The Z-normalization values of the target metrics 1, 2 and 3 are shown in Fig. 3.

3.2   Outlier Detection

The data collected from production processes may possess abnormalities due to several reasons such as environmental factors, various operator-generated problems during production, or improper data collection because of system/sensor failures. For this reason, it is helpful to flag abnormal records before proceeding to model the building and prediction phases. Following this, each dataset is separated into clusters using Local Outlier Factor (LOF) method [4] in order to get the most suitable models for the natural (normal) and unnatural (unusual) characteristics of the manufacturing process. LOF score is equal to the ratio of the average local density of the k-nearest neighbors of the instance and the local

Table 2. Feature summary statistics of the plastic dataset.

Feature	Mean	Std	CoV	Min	Max	Feature	Mean	Std	CoV	Min	Max
0	1.0	0.1	0.1	0.9	1.2	23	229.1	6.4	0.0	188.1	240.0
1	116.3	4.9	0.0	101.2	131.3	24	229.1	6.3	0.0	188.1	240.2
2	56.0	9.7	0.2	34.4	80.0	25	223.9	7.6	0.0	182.2	234.9
3	334.2	43.3	0.1	233.6	445.7	26	196.7	7.6	0.0	175.1	215.8
4	16.7	9.3	0.6	−0.3	34.9	27	178.6	4.8	0.0	154.9	190.3
5	229.6	16.4	0.1	157.2	274.3	28	226.2	8.3	0.0	184.1	239.7
6	549.8	44.2	0.1	11.7	634.9	29	241.7	7.0	0.0	197.8	254.6
7	152.0	9.9	0.1	110.7	182.8	30	242.5	6.9	0.0	198.5	255.6
8	185.2	17.1	0.1	107.9	278.8	31	235.3	8.2	0.0	190.3	248.3
9	45.4	4.2	0.1	25.3	59.0	32	206.0	9.0	0.0	186.0	230.7
10	52.9	4.6	0.1	2.1	61.3	33	183.8	5.9	0.0	160.0	199.0
11	19.0	0.8	0.0	11.9	19.9	34	224.5	8.1	0.0	182.9	238.1
12	4.9	0.4	0.1	3.9	6.6	35	238.5	6.8	0.0	195.4	251.0
13	200.7	8.8	0.0	181.7	227.6	36	238.0	6.7	0.0	195.0	250.5
14	168.4	8.9	0.1	145.7	199.5	37	231.4	7.9	0.0	187.9	243.7
15	46.8	4.9	0.1	35.2	56.5	38	202.0	8.4	0.0	181.5	224.8
16	35.6	3.9	0.1	27.2	43.6	39	182.4	5.5	0.0	158.6	196.6
17	1815.0	62.5	0.0	815.5	1840.0	40	685.1	46.6	0.1	390.2	830.4
18	1182.1	861.0	0.7	0.0	1834.8	41	3.4	0.3	0.1	2.9	6.2
19	1812.0	142.6	0.1	0.0	1853.0	42	1958.3	134.2	0.1	1830.0	2100.0
20	1768.6	274.8	0.2	0.0	1836.9	43	18.1	0.6	0.0	8.2	18.3
21	1810.2	109.9	0.1	0.0	1840.9	44	68.2	5.9	0.1	32.5	83.2
22	224.5	8.1	0.0	182.9	238.1	45	587.3	16.8	0.0	323.7	675.9

density of the data instance itself [5]. Groups with a significantly lower LOF score are specified as "unusual" segment. In this study, the number of neighbors, k, is assumed as 10.

According to this segmentation approach, the textile dataset turns out to have 1431 points in the normal segment and 80 points in the unusual segment. We also divide the normal segment into training and testing sets, which have 1,144 and 287 data points, respectively. On the other hand, the plastic dataset contains 399 points in the normal segment (287 in training and 72 in the test set) and 40 points in the unusual segment.

In the next sections, feature selection for the normal segment of each dataset is provided along with the predictive performance of the RFR method. The analysis is carried out in two major steps: first, the analysis regarding the "normal" data is presented. Then, the analysis is provided for the "unusual" data, for which the ensemble of regressor chains significantly outperforms the single target models.

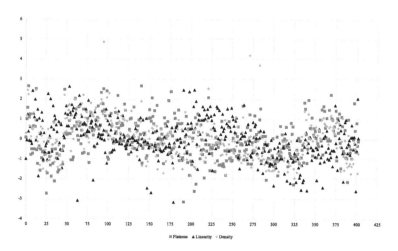

Fig. 3. Z-normalization scores of the plastic dataset target variables [14].

3.3   Feature Selection

Feature selection is one of the most crucial steps in developing learners. We perform feature selection procedure consisting of several steps, first of which is constructing feature importance graphs (presented in Fig. 4) for each target variable.

According to the feature importance analysis, it is observed that top three features explain more than 80% of variability for water permeability and abrasion resistance; where as this ratio falls below 50% for the tear strength. Another important observation is that the most influential feature in explaining variability in water permeability accounts for 75% of the variability in the response. Based on this first analysis, it can be said that the learner that is going to be developed in order to predict tear strength will be more complex compared to learners of the other two response variables.

In the plastic dataset, on the other hand, a pre-selection is conducted by comparing the minimum, maximum and equal values of the features. In addition to this selection, highly correlated signals are detected using Pearson correlation coefficient and the features to be dropped (among the correlated features) are selected by consulting the area experts. Moreover, some of the features, which express the same main feature, are combined using average or median calculations. For example, temperature measurements taken from different points of a surface are combined by averaging in order to express a single temperature value for the surface. After these feature elimination steps, there remains 22 features for the plastic dataset. The of which, importance graphs are shown in Fig. 5.

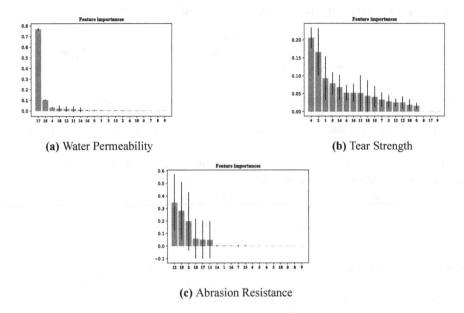

Fig. 4. Feature importance graphs for textile dataset [14]. Plot presents feature importance values for all three targets, namely water permeability, tear strength and abrasion resistance.

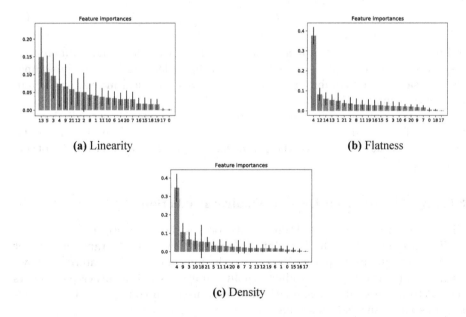

Fig. 5. Feature importance for plastic.

3.4   Implementation and Analysis Methods

In the first step of the numerical analysis, single-target regression models are created for each metric in the "normal" dataset. Then, the best performing single-target regression model is selected and compared with the ERC model. During the comparison, we use MAPE as the key performance metric and conduct a set of statistical tests/analyses, which are vector comparison, paired t-test, and one-way ANOVA test. In the second step, a similar comparison between the single-target regression model and ERC is conducted using the "unusual" dataset.

For the sake of completeness, we present the details of the metrics, statistical tests, and analysis we use during the comparison.

MAPE is calculated by the following equation:

$$MAPE = \frac{1}{n} \sum_i \frac{|\hat{y}_i - y_i|}{|y_i|}, \tag{1}$$

where y_i is actual value of sample i and $\hat{y}_i$ is prediction of sample i.

In paired t-test, the mean of the observed values for a variable from two dependent samples are paired and compared. As we use different algorithms to predict the same set of data points, pairing is direct possible as a natural consequence of the process. The test is used to decide whether the sample means compared are identical or not. The differences between all pairs are calculated by the following equation:

$$t = \frac{\bar{X}_D - \mu_0}{\frac{s_D}{\sqrt{n}}}, \tag{2}$$

where $\bar{X}_D$ and s_D are the mean and standard deviation of those differences, respectively. The constant μ_0 equals to zero if the underlying hypothesis assumes the two samples are coming from populations with identical means, and n represents the number of pairs.

In vector comparison analysis, algorithms are scored for their prediction performance for each data point separately. The algorithm yielding the minimum absolute percentage error for the given data point receives 1 (winner), others receive 0.

3.5   A Model-Driven DSS for Quality Prediction

The proposed DSS consists of four main modules showed in Fig. 6.

The first module is the User Interface where the system parameters are set and the outputs are displayed to manage the information. This interface allows users to enter the type of product, quality limits, as well as other parameters related to manufacturing. Similarly, the main user can configure database connections and visualization settings.

The second one is the Data Module which stores the manufacturing signal information needed to predict quality in the relational database. To elaborate,

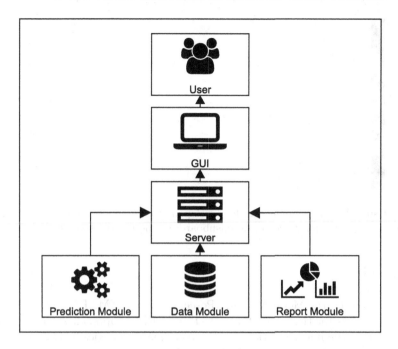

Fig. 6. Schematic view of the decision support system.

some of the information stored in this section, including selected signals, pre-prepared signal time mapping scenarios, and laboratory results. Previously created settings or predictive models are also stored in the database. In the designed system, different users can be defined and separate database records are kept for each user.

The third module is the Prediction Module that contains the model for quality prediction and feature selection. The models are implemented in Python 3.7.

Finally, the fourth module is the Report Module that creates a progression of administration reports after batch completed or new laboratory results produced. It can present reports for comparison of the results produced by the prediction module and actual quality measurements from the laboratory.

The DSS structure works as follows:

- The live process data are read from a programmable logic controller (PLC) via Open Platform Communications (OPC) and recorded on the database.
- The system gives predictions using the live data with pre-trained models on the database, and record the results on the database.
- The results are displayed live on the web via Grafana (Fig. 7). Grafana [7] is one of the popular free open-source visualization and monitoring tools that work as a web application to create dashboards and graphics and supports various data sources.
- This process is repeated at a predetermined frequency.

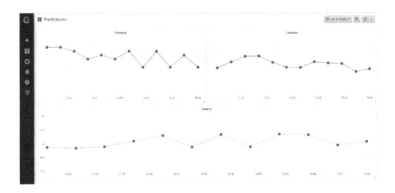

Fig. 7. A snapshot to demonstrate the developed graphical user interface of DSS. The interface show the quality prediction dashboard for the plastic dataset.

4   Results

In this section, firstly, Mean Absolute Percentage Error (MAPE) values of training and test sets for the single target (ST) and ERC approaches are presented. In order to see the linear relationship between quality metrics, correlation tables are also provided. Then the effect of the ERC approach on the performance of the quality metrics of both datasets is presented.

Random Forest Regressor is used as a single-target model for both datasets. In Table 3, test and train errors are given for textile dataset. In this table, Metric 3 shows the best test performance in the textile dataset, while Metric 2 shows the worst performance. In other words, with the ERC approach will be used, it is seen that there is a possibility of improvement for Metric 2 and Metric 3.

Table 3. MAPE results for textile dataset [14].

	Train	Test
Metric 1	0.011	0.020
Metric 2	0.030	0.045
Metric 3	0.002	0.003

As it can be clearly seen from the Table 4, it is understood that there is no direct linear relationship between the three quality metrics.

In the plastic dataset, according to Table 5, test and train errors are very close to each other but there is a possibility to improve Metric 1 and Metric 3 by ERC approach. In the correlation table (Table 6), it is seen that there is a significant correlation between Metric 1 and Metric 3, and this correlation may lead to an improvement in the predictive performance of Metric 1 which has the worst results in MAPE table, by the advantage of the chain approach in ERC.

Table 4. Correlation matrix of output variables for textile [14].

	Metric 1	Metric 2	Metric 3
Metric 1	1	−0.019	0.018
Metric 2	−0.019	1	−0.200
Metric 3	0.018	−0.200	1

Table 5. MAPE results for plastic dataset.

	Train	Test
Metric 1	0.039	0.062
Metric 2	0.032	0.042
Metric 3	0.035	0.054

Table 6. Correlation matrix of output variables for plastic.

	Metric 1	Metric 2	Metric 3
Metric 1	1	−0.037	0.665
Metric 2	−0.037	1	0.236
Metric 3	0.665	0.236	1

After obtaining single target results, the ERC approach emerged as an opportunity to improve the predictive performances of the relatively disadvantageous quality metrics in both datasets by revealing linear or nonlinear relationships between target variables. With the ERC approach, it is possible to evaluate both input and output variables together, thereby unveiling the dependencies and inner relationships that have a positive impact on predictive performance [1]. Because we have a small number of target variables for both datasets, regression models are trained by implementing the ERC framework for all possible chain sequences, and the mean of the predicted values are reported as final predictions for each quality metric.

MAPE comparison, vector comparison and paired t-test results are shown in Table 7 and Table 8 for textile dataset.

Table 7. ERC vs ST performance comparison for textile dataset [14].

	MAPE		Vector	
	ERC	ST	ERC	ST
Metric 1	0.019	0.020	159	129
Metric 2	0.042	0.045	150	138
Metric 3	0.003	0.003	133	155

Table 8. ERC vs ST residuals t-test Comparison for testing. $R_i{}^j$ represents residual vector of algorithm i for metric j in textile dataset [14].

Residuals	p-Value
$R_{ERC}{}^1 - R_{ST}{}^1$	0.115
$R_{ERC}{}^2 - R_{ST}{}^2$	0.025
$R_{ERC}{}^3 - R_{ST}{}^3$	0.382

For the textile dataset, according to Table 7, in the prediction of Metric 1 and Metric 2 respectively, the ERC method offers %5 and %4.5 improvement over ST results. The benefit of ERC for the Metric 1 and 2 ERC method is also apparent in the vector comparison test. Although there is not much improvement in the MAPE value for Metric 3, the number of better-predicted results increased compared to ST model. This is because the error value found for Metric 3 is already too low and has reached its natural limits. Table 8 indicates that there is no evidence to conclude that in the prediction of Metric 1 and 3, the ERC model is superior to the ST regressors since the p-values for the test statistics of residual vectors are greater than the conventional significance level threshold of 0.05. Besides, in the comparison of the residuals of Metric 2, it can be said that the ERC approach provides a statistically significant improvement since the p-value is below the 0.05 significance level.

MAPE comparison, vector comparison and paired t-test results are shown in Table 9 and Table 10 for plastic dataset.

Table 9. ERC vs ST performance comparison for plastic dataset.

	MAPE		Vector	
	ERC	ST	ERC	ST
Metric 1	0.054	0.062	40	32
Metric 2	0.039	0.042	38	34
Metric 3	0.044	0.054	41	31

Table 10. ERC vs ST residuals t-test Comparison for testing. $R_i{}^j$ represents residual vector of algorithm i for metric j.

Residuals	p-Value
$R_{ERC}{}^1 - R_{ST}{}^1$	0
$R_{ERC}{}^2 - R_{ST}{}^2$	0.353
$R_{ERC}{}^3 - R_{ST}{}^3$	0.029

In the plastic dataset, ERC approach gives better results in the predictive performance of all metrics as it is seen in both MAPE and vector comparisons. According to MAPE comparison, the improvements obtained for Metric 1, 2, and 3 are %13, %7, and %19, respectively. As reported by the residual analysis, there is a statistically significant difference between the predictive models of ERC and ST models for Metric 1 and Metric 3 because the p-values are below 0.05. In other words, it can be said that ERC model provides significant improvements for Metric 1 and 3.

In the second phase of the analysis, the predictive performances of the models trained with the normal dataset in the unusual dataset are discussed. Since the unusual dataset is different from the general production characteristic, it is evident that models trained with the normal dataset will perform worse in this dataset. However, with the ERC approach, the predictive performance of the target variables, which are more disadvantageous than the normal set performance, can be improved.

Comparison results for the unusual segment of the textile dataset are presented in Table 11 and Table 12.

Table 11. ERC vs ST MAPE comparison for textile dataset unusual segment [14].

	MAPE		Vector	
	ERC	ST	ERC	ST
Metric 1	0.027	0.029	43	37
Metric 2	0.127	0.138	51	29
Metric 3	0.004	0.004	44	36

Table 12. ERC vs ST residuals t-test Comparison for textile dataset unusual segment [14].

Residuals	p-Value
$R_{ERC}{}^{1} - R_{ST}{}^{1}$	0.006
$R_{ERC}{}^{2} - R_{ST}{}^{2}$	0
$R_{ERC}{}^{3} - R_{ST}{}^{3}$	0.078

When MAPE and residual analysis with the 0.05 significance level is considered, it can be said that significant improvements have been achieved for Metric 1 and Metric 2 at %6.9 and %8, respectively. According to vector comparison, ERC yields higher prediction performance in two-thirds of the dataset. Since the predictive performances for Metric 3 are still very close to its natural limit, no improvement could be achieved and no significant difference is observed between the prediction models.

MAPE comparison, vector comparison and paired t-test results for the plastic dataset are shown in Table 13 and Table 14.

Table 13. ERC vs ST Mape Comparison for plastic dataset unusual segment.

	MAPE		Vector	
	ERC	ST	ERC	ST
Metric 1	0.055	0.057	24	16
Metric 2	0.034	0.036	23	17
Metric 3	0.038	0.048	27	13

Table 14. ERC vs ST residuals t-test Comparison for plastic dataset unusual segment.

Residuals	p-Value
$R_{ERC}^{\;1} - R_{ST}^{\;1}$	0.005
$R_{ERC}^{\;2} - R_{ST}^{\;2}$	0.129
$R_{ERC}^{\;3} - R_{ST}^{\;3}$	0.955

According to the performance results of unusual segment of the plastic dataset, %4, %26, and %21 better error values are obtained for the three metrics respectively. The same result is seen in the vector comparison table. Vector comparison indicates ERC approach gives higher prediction performance in two-thirds of the dataset. However, when the residual analysis is the case, it is observed that there is a significant difference between ST and ERC models for only Metric 1 because of p-values of other models' residuals are greater than the 0.05 significance level.

5   Conclusion

In this paper, we proposed a web-based decision support system using ensemble machine learning algorithms in order to predict the quality level of products in different manufacturing settings. Two different datasets are used for the analysis and they are segmented as "normal" and "unusual" clusters via the local outlier factor method. The normal cluster refers to the usual pattern of the data, and the unusual one refers to the unusual pattern compared to expected process data. Then, single target regression and ERC approaches are applied to predict quality metrics of the last product, and performances of the algorithms are compared. As a result, it is seen that the ERC approach provided significant improvements in 2 metrics in the first dataset, and 1 metric in the second dataset and outperformed

ST regression. In unusual sets, it is observed that the prediction performance decreased significantly. Hence, a regressor-based ensemble algorithm is proposed as a solution that achieves better predictive efficiency in two-thirds of these datasets. Besides, developed web-based DSS structure enables that the applied predictive approaches can be made available for industrial facilities in real-time and the operators are given the opportunity to intervene immediately against the observed abnormalities in production processes and quality decreases due to production setup. Thus, it helps to reduce production defects that are outside the predetermined quality limits.

As future work, proposed DSS, which will be developed with the feedback from live tests, will be turned into a machine learning-based recommendation engine. This will enable the operator to operate the system at the recommended production settings in accordance with the predetermined quality targets. After the second phase is successful, the recommendation engine will be plugged into PLC and begin to change the set parameters of the machine as part of the automation system. With the completion of the targeted steps, the industrial facilities will have their first full-scaled industry 4.0 applications.

References

1. Borchani, H., Varando, G., Bielza, C., Larrañaga, P.: A survey on multi-output regression. Wiley Interdisc. Rev. Data Min. Knowl. Discov. **5**(5), 216–233 (2015)
2. Borodin, V., Bourtembourg, J., Hnaien, F., Labadie, N.: Handling uncertainty in agricultural supply chain management: a state of the art. Eur. J. Oper. Res. **254**(2), 348–359 (2016)
3. Breiman, L.: Random forests. Mach. Learn. **45**(1), 5–32 (2001)
4. Breunig, M.M., Kriegel, H.P., Ng, R.T., Sander, J.: Lof: identifying density-based local outliers. In: ACM sigmod record. vol. 29, pp. 93–104. ACM (2000)
5. Chandola, V., Banerjee, A., Kumar, V.: Anomaly detection: a survey. ACM Comput. Surv. (CSUR) **41**(3), 15 (2009)
6. Felsberger, A., Oberegger, B., Reiner, G.: A review of decision support systems for manufacturing systems. In: SAMI@ iKNOW (2016)
7. Grafana Labs: Grafana documentation (2018). https://grafana.com/docs/
8. Ivlev, I., Vacek, J., Kneppo, P.: Multi-criteria decision analysis for supporting the selection of medical devices under uncertainty. Eur. J. Oper. Res. **247**(1), 216–228 (2015)
9. Li, B., Li, J., Li, W., Shirodkar, S.A.: Demand forecasting for production planning decision-making based on the new optimised fuzzy short time-series clustering. Prod. Plann. Control **23**(9), 663–673 (2012)
10. Mansouri, S.A., Gallear, D., Askariazad, M.H.: Decision support for build-to-order supply chain management through multiobjective optimization. Int. J. Prod. Econ. **135**(1), 24–36 (2012)
11. Noordin, M.N.: Sink marks defect on injection molding using different raw materials. Ph.D. thesis, UMP (2009)
12. Pourabdollahi, Z., Karimi, B., Mohammadian, A.K., Kawamura, K.: Shipping chain choices in long-distance supply chains: descriptive analysis and decision tree model. Transp. Res. Rec. **2410**(1), 58–66 (2014)

13. Power, D.J., Sharda, R.: Model-driven decision support systems: concepts and research directions. Decis. Support Syst. **43**(3), 1044–1061 (2007)
14. Sahin, A., Demirel, K.C., Albey, E., Gürsun, G.: International roaming traffic optimization with call quality. In: Hammoudi, S., Quix, C., Bernardino, J. (eds.) Proceedings of the 8th International Conference on Data Science, Technology and Applications, DATA 2019, Prague, Czech Republic, 26–28 July 2019, pp. 92–99. SciTePress (2019)
15. Spyromitros-Xioufis, E., Tsoumakas, G., Groves, W., Vlahavas, I.: Multi-label classification methods for multi-target regression, pp. 1159–1168 (2012). arXiv preprint arXiv:1211.6581

Farm Area Segmentation in Satellite Images Using DeepLabv3+ Neural Networks

Sara Sharifzadeh$^{1(\boxtimes)}$ ⓘ, Jagati Tata^1, Hilda Sharifzadeh^3, and Bo Tan^2 ⓘ

^{1} Coventry University, Coventry CV1 2JH, UK
ac8115@Coventry.ac.uk
^{2} Tampere University, Tampere, Finland
^{3} University of Warwick, Coventry CV4 7AL, UK

Abstract. Farm detection using low resolution satellite images is an important part of digital agriculture applications such as crop yield monitoring. However, it has not received enough attention compared to high-resolution images. Although high resolution images are more efficient for detection of land cover components, the analysis of low-resolution images are yet important due to the low-resolution repositories of the past satellite images used for timeseries analysis, free availability and economic concerns. In this paper, semantic segmentation of farm areas is addressed using low resolution satellite images. The segmentation is performed in two stages; First, local patches or Regions of Interest (ROI) that include farm areas are detected. Next, deep semantic segmentation strategies are employed to detect the farm pixels. For patch classification, two previously developed local patch classification strategies are employed; a two-step semi-supervised methodology using hand-crafted features and Support Vector Machine (SVM) modelling and transfer learning using the pretrained Convolutional Neural Networks (CNNs). For the latter, the high-level features learnt from the massive filter banks of deep Visual Geometry Group Network (VGG-16) are utilized. After classifying the image patches that contain farm areas, the DeepLabv3+ model is used for semantic segmentation of farm pixels. Four different pretrained networks, resnet18, resnet50, resnet101 and mobilenetv2, are used to transfer their learnt features for the new farm segmentation problem. The first step results show the superiority of the transfer learning compared to hand-crafted features for classification of patches. The second step results show that the model trained based on resnet50 achieved the highest semantic segmentation accuracy.

Keywords: Farm detection · Semantic segmentation · Satellite image

1 Introduction

Satellite image analysis is an important topic in land cover classification and remote sensing domain. In digital agriculture, farm detection is a key factor for different agricultural applications such as diagnosis of diseases and welfare-impairments, crop yield monitoring and surveillance and control of micro-environmental conditions [1–4].

© Springer Nature Switzerland AG 2020
S. Hammoudi et al. (Eds.): DATA 2019, CCIS 1255, pp. 115–135, 2020.
https://doi.org/10.1007/978-3-030-54595-6_7

While new high-resolution satellites are launched every day, it is still important to study and use Low-resolution satellite imagery that is being used since more than 30 years. That is due to the fact that the increased resolution offered by new sensors improve the accuracy and precision, yet the continuity of the existing low-resolution systems data is crucial for time series analysis. One important application of time series investigation is change detection, that requires comparison with low resolution images of the old databases [5, 6]. Another example of using low-resolution satellite images for crop monitoring and yield forecasting is [7], that uses Landsat imagery in order to expand the used operational systems. Furthermore, the processing time and cost of analyzing high resolution satellite images is more [8], while the variations in sensor angle and increase in shadows might influence the accuracy when using high resolution sensors [8]. Such factors challenge the precision of spatial rectification. Then, a compromise between accuracy and cost should be considered for the resolution of the satellite images depending on the application. Therefore, for land cover classification and semantic segmentation of large features such as farms, low resolution satellite images for instance, Landsat are appropriate [3].

Image segmentation methods address the problem of finding objects boundaries in images. This leads to assigning multiple sets of pixels in an image into different classes or objects [9].

There is a long history for land cover classification and semantic segmentation of meaningful objects from the scene. In early works, when pixels were bigger than ground features due to very low resolution [10, 11], pixels, sub-pixel or object level analysis were carried out using unsupervised and supervised techniques such as Neural Networks (NN), decision trees and nearest neighbors and hybrid classification [12–17]. Then, due to the significant increase in spatial resolution of images, objects include several pixels. Therefore, Object-Based Image Analysis (OBIA) was developed for the improved spatial resolution of images [11] to deal with complex classes [18]. OBIA assigns groups of pixels into shapes with a meaningful representation of objects [10]. For this aim, usually image segmentation is performed followed by feature extraction and classification. The segmentation step is more critical and influences the overall accuracy [19, 20].

In many cases software and computational tools such as ERDAS and Khoros 2.2 were used [17]. eCognition and ArcGIS softwares are recent examples in this case [8, 21]; Traditional hand-crafted feature extraction and discrimination techniques for object classification in remote sensing was reviewed in [22]. When using low resolution images such as Landsat 8, appropriate choice of training samples, segmentation parameters and modelling strategy is important. That is a challenge in using software-based strategies and limit their accuracy [21]. An example in this case is selection of a suitable segmentation scale to avoid over and under segmentation in Object Based Image Analysis OBIA. Although there are several reports of superior performance on different landscapes, due to the segmentation scale issue and lower resolution, OBIA is not very ideal for Landsat data [21].

Utilization of saliency maps for pixel level classification of high-resolution satellite images was performed based on spectral domain analysis such as Fourier and wavelet transforms for creation of local and global saliency maps [23, 24]. In another work based on saliency analysis low level SIFT descriptors, middle-level features using locality-constrained linear coding (LLC) and high level features using deep Boltzmann machine (DBM) were combined [25].

In addition, the state of the art CNNs have been used recently for classification of satellite images [26–28]. Due to the limited effectiveness of manual low-level feature extraction methods in highly varying and complex images such as diverse range of land coverage in satellite images, deep feature learning strategies have been applied recently for ground coverage detection problems. One of the effective deep learning strategies is the deep CNNs due to its bank of convolutional filters that enables quantification of massive high-level spectral and spatial features. For semantic segmentation problems, the most recently developed methods are based on deep learning techniques [29]. Examples of such techniques are fully convolutional network (FCN) [30–33], encoder-decoder architectures such as Unet [34] and other similar architectures such as an subsample-upsample architecture in [35], LinkNet [36], ResNet [37], AD-LinkNet [29]. Recently. deepLabv3 [38] and deepLabv3+ [39] methods based on atrous convolution have been developed for semantic segmentation.

In this paper, the problem of farm detection and segmentation using low resolution satellite images is addressed. In our previous contribution, a farm detection strategy was developed at patch level [40]. The analysis include two different strategies; the first one was a semi-supervised strategy based on hand-crafted features combined by classification modeling similar to [40–43]. The developed algorithm consists of an unsupervised pixel-based segmentation of vegetation area using Normalized Difference Moisture Index (NDMI), followed by a supervised step for texture area classification and farm detection; GLCM and 2-D DCT features are used in an SVM framework for texture classification and then, object-based morphological features were extracted from the textured areas for farm detection. The second one was a CNN-based transfer learning strategy that uses the pre-trained VGGNet16 for local patch classification.

The main contribution of this paper is segmentation of farm areas semantically at pixel level. The analysis strategy consists of two main stages; first similar to our previous work [40], local image patches or ROIs that include farm areas are detected. Then, having found the local ROIs consisting the farm areas, in the next step, semantic segmentation of farm regions in the ROIs is performed using deepLabv3+ modelling strategy [39]. Based on transfer learning concept, labelled ROIs including farms are used together with four different pretrained networks, resnet18, resnet50, resnet101 and mobilenet and the transferred models results are compared.

The rest of paper is organized as follows; Sect. 2 is about data description. Section 3 describes the both classification strategies. The experimental results are presented in Sect. 4 and we finally conclude in Sect. 5.

2 Dara Description

Landsat 8 is the latest earth imaging satellite of the Landsat Program operated by the EROS Data Centre of United States Geological Survey (USGS), in collaboration with NASA. The spatial resolution of the images is 30 m. Landsat 8 captures more than 700 scenes per day. The instruments Operational Land Imager (OLI) and Thermal Infrared

Sensor (TIRS) in Landsat 8 have improved Signal to Noise Ratio (SNR). The products downloaded are 16-bit images (55,000 grey levels) [3, 44]. There are 11 bands out of which, the visible and infrared (IR) bands are used in this paper. The data set consist Landsat 8 image of an area near Tendales, Ecuador (See Fig. 1). In this work, different combinations of band are used for calculating vegetation and moisture indices used in estimation of vegetation green areas as well as visible RGB bands for classification analysis.

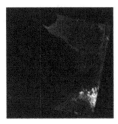

Fig. 1. Landsat 8 RGB image of Tendales, Ecuador. (Color Figure Online)

3   Methodology

In this section the procedures used for classification of farm patches and segmentation of farm areas in the detected patch are described. Figure 2 shows the overall analysis strategy in this work.

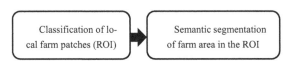

Fig. 2. Overall analysis strategy of this paper.

3.1   Classification of Patches (ROIs)

Two strategies are used and compared in this paper for classification of local patches of satellite image into farm and non-farm. They are described in the following.

Hand-Crafted Features for Classification of Farm Patches. First, the vegetation area is segmented using the NDMI image. Next, local patches are generated automatically, from the segmented green area. Then, textured areas including farms or any other pattern are classified by applying SVM on the extracted features using GLCM and 2-D DCT. Finally, the farm areas are detected by morphological analysis of the textured patches and SVM modelling. MATLAB 2018 was used for all implementations. Figure 3 shows the block diagram of the analysis strategy.

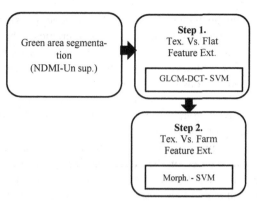

Fig. 3. Block diagram showing the overall classification process based on hand-crafted features.

Vegetation Segmentation. There are two standard indexes for segmentation of green vegetation area. They are Normalized Difference Vegetation Index (NDVI) [45] and NDMI [46]. The pixels are segmented using spectral bands; the Near Infra-Red (NIR) in 851–879 nm range and Shortwave NIR (SWIR) in 1566–1651 nm range. However, NDMI [46] is a more suitable technique because it considers the moisture content of the soil and plants instead of the leaf chlorophyll content or leaf area. There are also similar works like [47], which have used NDMI and tasseled cap transformations on 30 m resolution Landsat images for estimating soil moisture. Hence, the farm areas that went undetected by NDVI are well detected by thresholded NDMI strategy. NDMI uses two near-infrared bands (one channel of 1.24-μm that was never used previously for vegetation indices) to identify the soil moisture content. It is employed in forestry and agriculture applications [48]. This index has been used in this paper for the estimation of total vegetation including the agricultural lands and farms. For Lands imagery, NDMI is calculated as:

$$NDMI = \frac{NIR - SWIR}{NIR + SWIR} \qquad (1)$$

NDMI is always in the range $[-1, +1]$. It is reported that NDMI values more than 0.10–0.20 indicate very wet or moist soil surfaces [46]. Then, based on this study, cultivable land is extracted for further classification.

Texture Area Detection. The detected green areas from the previous step are mapped on the RGB band images. Farm areas are part of the green areas of the image; therefore, the detected green areas are divided into small patches of 200×200 pixels. Then, feature extraction is performed for each patch of image to detect the textured patches. Patches with flat patterns do not include a farm area.

GLCM - One of the feature extraction techniques employed for texture areas is the GLCM that is widely used for texture analysis [49]. The GLCM studies the spatial correlation of the pixel grayscale and spatial relationship between the pixels separated by some distance in the image. It looks for regional consistency considering the extent and direction of grey level variation. Considering the characteristics of the flat regions and the textured regions (non-farm or farm) as shown in Fig. 4. GLCM is used for discrimination. Mathematically, the spatial relation of pixels in image matrix is quantified by computing how often different combinations of grey levels co-occur in the image or a section of the image. For example, how often a pixel with intensity or tone value i occurs either horizontally, vertically, or diagonally to another pixel at distance d with the value j (see Fig. 5-a). Depending on the range of intensities in an image, a number of scales are defined and a GLCM square matrix of the same dimensional size is formed. Then, image pixels are quantized based on the discrete scales and the GLCM matrix is filled for each direction. Figure 5-b shows the formation process of a GLCM matrix based on horizontal occurrences at $d = 1$. The grayscales are between 1 to maximums 8 in this case.

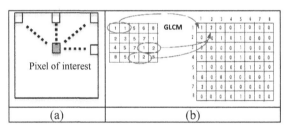

(a)   (b)   (c)

Fig. 4. Examples of (a) Flat (b) Textured-farm (c) Textured non-farm patches [40].

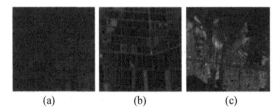

(a)   (b)

Fig. 5. (a) Illustration of forming GLCM matrices in four directions i.e., $0°, 45°, 90°, 135°$. (b) Computation of GLCM matrix based on horizontal occurrences at $d = 1$ for an image [50].

Two order statistical parameters: Contrast, Correlation, Energy and Homogeneity samples are used to define texture features in the vegetation. Considering a grey co-occurrence matrix p, they are defined as:

$$\text{Contrast} = \sum_{i,j} |i - j|^2 p(i, j) \tag{2}$$

$$\text{Correlation} = \sum_{i,j} \frac{(i - \mu_i)(j - \mu_j)p(i, j)}{\sigma_i \sigma_j} \tag{3}$$

$$\text{Energy} = \sum_{i,j} p(i,j)^2 \tag{4}$$

$$\text{Homogenity} = \sum_{i,j} \frac{p(i,j)}{1 + |i-j|} \tag{5}$$

where, i, j denote row and column number, μ_i, μ_j, σ_i, σ_j are the means and standard deviations of p_x and p_y, so that, $p_x(i) = \sum_{j=0}^{G-1} p(i,j)$ and $p_y(j) = \sum_{i=0}^{G-1} p(i,j)$. G is the number of intensity scales, used for GLCM matrix formation.

Further detailed information can be found in [51]. The GLCM features are calculated in directions $0°, 45°, 90°$, and $135°$ as shown in Fig. 2-a. The calculated GLCM features in the four directions are averaged for each parameter and used as input to the classification model $\text{GLCM} = [\text{Cont}_{av}, \text{Corr}_{av}, \text{Eng}_{av}, \text{Hom}_{av}]$.

2D DCT - DCT sorts the spatial frequency of an image in ascending order and in the form of cosine coefficients. Most significant coefficients lie in the lower order, corresponding to the main components of the image, while the higher order coefficients correspond to high variation in images. Since the variation in a textured patch is higher than a flat one, the DCT map can help to distinguish them. For this aim, the original image patch I_{org} is transformed into DCT domain I_{DCT} and a hard threshold is applied to the DCT coefficients to remove the high order coefficients $I_{DCT(th)}$. Then, the inverse 2D-DCT of the thresholded image I_{iDCT} is computed. In both original and DCT domain, the reduction in the entropy of the textured patches is more significant than the flat areas representing smooth variations. Therefore, the ratio of coefficients' entropy before and after thresholding $\left[\frac{ent(I_{DCT})}{ent(I_{DCT(th)})}, \frac{ent(I_{org})}{ent(I_{iDCT})} \right]$ are calculated in both domains. For textured patches the entropy ratios are greater compared to flat patches due to the significant drop in entropy after thresholding the large amount of high frequency information.

Morphological Features. To recognize if a detected textured patch contains farm areas, first the patch image is converted to grayscale image. Then, the Sobel edge detection followed by morphological opening and closing by reconstruction are performed. This highlights the farm areas, keeping the boundaries and shapes in the image undisturbed. Next, the regional maxima were found to extract only the areas of maximum intensity (or the highlighted foreground regions). Further, the small stray blobs, disconnected or isolated pixels, and pixels having low contrast with the background in their neighborhood are discarded. This is because there is a contrast between the farm regions (marked as foreground) and their surrounding boundary pixels. The same procedure is performed for a non-farm sample. The area of the foreground as well as the entropy for a patch including farm is higher compared to a non-farm due to the higher number of connected foreground pixels.

SVM Modelling. SVM classifiers are trained using the four GLCM and the two DCT features at step 1 and morphological features at step 2. The first model is capable to detect textured versus the flat patches and the second one detects the patches including farms from the textured patches with no farm areas. The LibSVM [52] is used. In this paper, the 5-fold cross-validation [53], is used to find the optimum kernel and the corresponding parameters. It helps to avoid over-fitting or under-fitting. The choice of kernel based on cross validation allows classifying data sets with both linear and non-linear behaviour. SVM was used for remote-sensing and hyperspectral image data analysis previously [54].

Transfer Learning Strategy for VGGNet16. CNN is a popular classification method based on deep learning of different levels of both spectral and special features using the stack of filter banks at several convolutional layers. However, training a CNN requires large data sets and heavy time-consuming computations and is prone to over-fitting using small data sets. A versatile approach in this case is transfer learning; The high-level deep features learnt over several layers of convolution, pooling and RELU using million images of massive ranges of scenes and objects are kept. That is based on the fact that the weighted combination of these activation maps of high-level features are the underlying building blocks of different objects of the scenes. While, the end layers called fully connected layers (FC) should be re-trained using hundreds of new training images. These layers are used to evaluate the strong correlation of the previous layers high-level features to particular classes of the task (in training images) and calculate the appropriate weights giving high probabilities for correct classifications. Figure 6 shows the transfer learning concept.

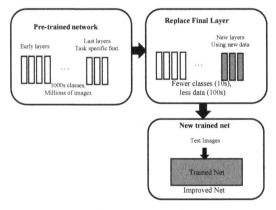

Fig. 6. Block diagram showing the transfer learning strategy [40].

The recent works on utilization of this technique [55, 56] shows suitability of transference of the learnt activation vectors for a new image classification task. Therefore, new patches of satellite images are used to retrain the final FC layers of VGG-16 CNN.

VGG-16 Network. The VGG-16 network is a pretrained network using more than a million images from the ImageNet database [57]. There are 16 deep layers and 1000 different classes of objects, e.g. keyboard, mouse, pencil, and many animals. This network has learned rich high-level feature representing wide ranges of objects. The size of input image is $224 \times 224 \times 3$ where the three color layers are RGB bands. The last three FC layers are trained for classification of 1000 classes. As explained, these three layers are retrained using our satellite image patches of the same size for farm classification while all other layers are kept.

3.2 Semantic Segmentation of Farm Area Using DeepLabv3+

As described in Introduction Section, after classifying the local patches, the pixels that include farm area are segmented. For this aim DeepLabv3+ model is used that utilizes an Encoder-Decoder architecture with atrous Convolution [39]. They are used in both DeepLabv3 and DeepLabv3+. They address two main challenges of semantic segmentation with deep CNN models, (1) the reduced feature resolution caused by consecutive pooling operations or convolution striding and (2) existence of objects at multiple scales [38].

The first challenge causes to learn increasingly abstract feature representations and invariance to local image transformation that makes issues in prediction tasks [38]. That is due to the loss of detailed spatial features that influences the prediction performance. To overcome this problem, atrous convolution also known as dilated convolution is used in both DeepLabv3 and DeepLabv3+ architecture. The resolution of extracted deep features can be controlled explicitly using atrous convolution (see Fig. 7). Given a two-dimensional image, for each location i on the output feature map y and a convolution filter w, atrous convolution is applied over the input feature map x according to the following equation:

$$y[i] = \sum_k x[i + rk]w[k]$$

where the atrous rate r determines the stride used to sample the input signal. If $r = 1$, it is the standard convolution.

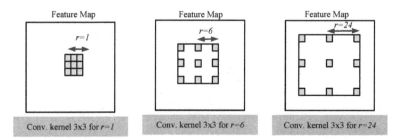

Fig. 7. Illustration of atrous convolution concept, with kernel size 3×3 and different rates. Standard convolution corresponds to atrous convolution with $r = 1$, while with higher atrous rates, the model's field-of-view enlarges and allows multi-scale feature extraction.

Using atrous also allows, adjusting the filter's field-of-view in order to capture multi-scale information which addresses the second challenge. Reviewing recent literatures shows that several methods have been proposed to address the issue with objects at multiple scales [58–61]. In DeepLabv3+, the spatial pyramid pooling is embedded into an encoder-decoder architecture as shown in Fig. 8. While the early layers include convolution and down-sampling operations (similar to Deep CNN), the down sampling operations are removed from the last few layers and instead, up-sampling of the corresponding filter kernels is performed and multiple parallel atrous convolutions are applied in different rates. This results in denser feature maps and capturing context at several ranges compared to Deep CNN (see Fig. 8).

As stated above, DeepLabv3+ utilizes an encoder-decoder structure. The encoder-decoder networks have been successfully used for different computer vision problems including semantic segmentation for example in [61, 62]. There are two main modules in encoder-decoder networks structure (1) an encoder module that gradually extracts semantic features and reduces the feature maps, and (2) a decoder module that gradually recovers the spatial information [39]. The encoder module that includes the spatial pyramid pooling has been described above. The last feature map in the top left side of Fig. 8 is the encoder output. The encoder features from DeepLabv3 [38] are usually computed with output stride $= 16$ and the features are then bilinearly up-sampled by a factor of 16. That is described as a naive decoding module and may not successfully recover object segmentation details [39]. Therefore, in DeepLabv3+, a simple yet effective decoder module is proposed as shown in Fig. 8 right side modules. Instead of up-sampling directly by a factor of 16, the encoder features are first bilinearly up-sampled by a factor of 4 and then concatenated with the corresponding low-level features from the left side encoder module that have the same spatial resolution. Then, few 3×3 convolutions followed by another simple bilinear up-sampling by a factor of 4 is performed. For further details, we refer to [39].

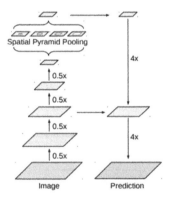

Fig. 8. The DeepLabv3+ encoder-decoder structure. The encoder module encodes multi-scale contextual information by applying atrous convolution at multiple scales, while the simple yet effective decoder module refines the segmentation results along object boundaries [39].

In this paper, four different pretrained networks, resnet18, resnet50, resnet101 and mobilenetv2, are used to transfer their learnt features into a DeepLabv3+ structure and train a new network for farm segmentation problem.

4 Experimental Results

In this section first the ROI classification results obtained from the both applied techniques, hand-crafted features and transfer learning using VGGNet16 will be presented. Then, the results of semantic segmentation of farm areas will be shown.

4.1 Hand-Crafted Features and Classification Modelling Results

Figure 9 shows the result of vegetation green area detection using NDMI. This image was further utilized for making patches (from green areas) that are used for the two-step classification framework.

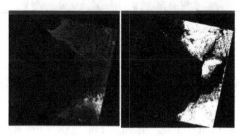

Fig. 9. (a) Landsat 8 image of Tendales, Ecuador (b) Result of thresholding using NDMI [40]. (Color Figure Online)

The number of training patches of both classes (textured verses flat and farm verses non- farm) were almost balanced at both feature extraction step and classification with SVM step. That is to avoid discriminative hyperplanes found by SVM that favors the more populated class. Totally from total patches, around 75% was used for training and the rest were kept as unseen data for test. In the first classification, 111 samples were used for training and 15 samples for test. In the second classification, there were 83 training samples and 22 test samples.

First, the four GLCM features and two DCT features were extracted from patches and combined. Figure 10 visualizes the 2D DCT maps of a flat and textured patch before thresholding the higher frequencies coefficients and after thresholding. As can be seen, the textured patch has high energies in both low frequencies as well as high frequencies, while in the flat patch DCT map, only low coefficients show high energy values. Therefore, the thresholded DCT map of the textured patch shows significant drop of energies in high frequencies. This influences the entropy ratios. Table 1 presents the average of the GLCM and DCT features over 20 patches for textured and flat classes. All the classified textured patches from this step were used to extract the morphology features at the second step, as shown in Fig. 11.

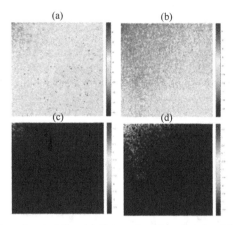

Fig. 10. DCT map before thresholding (a) flat patch, (b) textured patch. After thresholding (c) flat patch (d) textured patch [40].

Table 1. GLCM and one of the DCT features used for classification of Flat and Textured Areas. (values shown are averaged over 20 samples) [40].

Class	Cont.	Eng.	Hom.	Ent.	DCT Ent. Ratio
Flat	0.0041	0.991	0.9979	3.014	0.1202
Tex.	0.067	0.847	0.9671	4.761	0.3337

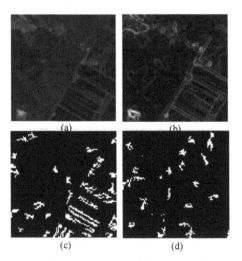

Fig. 11. (a) Grayscale image of a farm patch (b) Result of Sobel edge detection (c) Detected farm area by morphological foreground detection (d) Detected area of a textured non-farm patch shown in Fig. 4-c [40].

The performance of classifiers is evaluated based on the number of correctly classified samples. Results are presented in Table 2. As can be seen, the first texture classification step is very robust. However, the performance is reduced for the second farm classifier based on morphology features.

Table 2. Accuracy results of the two-step hand-crafted features and classification modelling strategy for farm detection [40].

Classification step	Train accuracy (%)	Test accuracy (%)
1	96.39 (107/111)	93.33 (14/15)
2	83.1325 (69/83)	81.8182 (18/22)

4.2 Transfer Learning Strategy Results

In order to retrain the three FC layers of VGG-16 net, hundreds of images are required. Then, further number of patches were used compared to the hand-crafted features and modelling strategy to fulfil the requirements of the second patch classification strategy. Transfer learning was performed using three different sets of more than 300 patches.

- The first set includes image patches from any general area of the satellite image, including ocean patches, mountains, residential areas, green flat and textured areas and farms. The last three FC layers of VGG-16 were retrained for the two-class farm detection problem.
- In the second set, the same number of patches were used excluding the non-green areas based on NDMI. This means the patches can include one of the flat green area, green textured non-farm area or a farm area.
- Finally, in the third set of the same size, only green textured non-farm patches as well as farm ones were used.

In all three cases, 75% of patches were used for training and the remaining was used as the test unseen data. There were 72 farm patches and the rest were non-farm in all three sets. Due to random selection, the number of patches of each class are different in the generated sets. The average and standard deviation of the results over 5 randomly generated train and test sets are reported in Table 3. As expected, no significant difference can be seen between the results of the three studies. That is, the high-level features acquired from the stack of filter banks include all those spectral, special, structural and color features extracted using the manual feature extraction strategy. Due to inclusive level of features extracted using the deep convolutional layers, the CNN results outperform the two-step feature extraction strategy.

Table 3. Average and standard deviation of the training and test accuracy of the CNN using transfer learning on the three different sets of patches [40].

Classification type	Train accuracy (%)	Test accuracy (%)
Farm vs. general areas	99.55 ± 0.64	96.76 ± 2.26
Farm vs. green areas	99.37 ± 0.76	95.95 ± 2.87
Farm vs. green tex. area	98.91 ± 0.52	96.76 ± 2.80

Figure 12 shows the confusion matrix of one of the five test sets results using the transferred CNN models. The first experiment data set, that classifies farm patches from any general patch was used. As shown, only one general non-farm patch was misclassified as a farm patch.

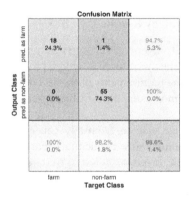

Fig. 12. The confusion matrix of one of the five test sets results from the first data set (classification of farm patches from any general patch) [40].

4.3 Semantic Segmentation of Farm Regions Results

In order to apply the semantic segmentation based on DeepLabv3+ the patch images pixels need to be labelled. That is due to the fact that it is supervised strategy and requires a label for every pixel of the image patch. For this aim, 72 local image patches that include farm areas in some parts were manually labelled. Totally seven different objects could be seen in the patch images and labelled accordingly. We refer to this data set as *Tendales_farm*. As we are only interested on farm area segmentation in this paper, all labels apart from farm are merged in this work and only two labels namely *farm* and *non-farm* are considered. Figure 13 shows sample patches and the corresponding labels.

In order to do semantic segmentation, the data set is divided into training (70%), validation (15%) and test sets (15%). Then DeepLabv+ network is considered using the four different pretrained networks, resnet18, resnet50, resnet101 and mobilenetv2. The

Fig. 13. Sample patches in Tendales_farm (top), the corresponding farm, non-farm labeled areas (down).

pixel classification layer was replaced based on farm classification problem classes and retrained using the training and validation images and their corresponding label sets. To compensate for class imbalance, the farm and non-farm classes weights are calculated. First the number of pixels in each class is calculated and divided by the total number of pixels, yielding 0.4029 and 0.5971 for the farm and non-farm classes. Then, the median of these frequencies is divided by the individual frequencies yielding the weights 1.2411, 0.8373 corresponding to the farm and non-farm classes. These weights are used in the cross entropy loss function that is used in the pixel classification layer. The Stochastic Gradient Descend with Momentum (SGDM) with piecewise learning rate was used for training. The number of epochs varied between 30 to 50 for the four models, and the training stopped afterwards due to no further improvements and to avoid overfitting.

In order to evaluate the performance of the models different metric factors are calculated. The first factor is accuracy. It is calculated for each class, based on the ratio of correctly classified pixels to the total number of pixels in that class, according to the ground truth. Given the number of True Positives (TP), False Positives (FP) and False Negatives (FN) as shown in Fig. 14, accuracy is calculated as follows:

$$Accuracy\ score = TP/(TP + FN) \tag{6}$$

It indicates how well each class correctly identifies pixels. Besides that, the global accuracy is calculated which is the ratio of correctly classified pixels, to the total number of pixels regardless of their class. This metric is computationally less expensive compared to each class accuracies.

Another metric is Intersection Over Union (IoU), that is also called *Jaccard similarity coefficient*. It is a statistical accuracy measurement that penalizes false positives and is

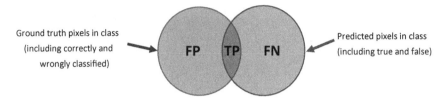

Ground truth pixels in class
(including correctly and
wrongly classified)

FP TP FN

Predicted pixels in class
(including true and false)

Fig. 14. Illustration of the relationship between TP, FP and FN.

commonly used. For each class, IoU is the ratio of correctly classified pixels to the total number of ground truth and predicted pixels in that class. Then, an IoU equal to one shows a perfect segmentation while an IoU smaller than one shows an increase in FP or FN.

$$IoU\ score = TP/(TP + FP + FN) \tag{7}$$

The training and test results obtained for the four different models are presented in Table 4 and 5. The most successful models in terms of global and class accuracy as well as the IoU factor are resnet18 and resnet50.

Table 4. Comparison of the four semantic segmentation models results on train set.

| Train set | Class accuracy | | Global accuracy | IoU | |
	Farm	Non-farm		Farm	Non-farm
resnet18	0.9411	0.8461	0.8854	0.7726	0.8123
resnet50	0.9413	0.8774	0.9038	0.8019	0.8425
resnet101	0.8942	0.8067	0.8429	0.7019	0.7507
mobilenetv2	0.8998	0.7972	0.8396	0.6989	0.7445

Table 5. Comparison of the four semantic segmentation models results on test set.

| Test set | Class accuracy | | Global accuracy | IoU | |
	Farm	Non-farm		Farm	Non-farm
resnet18	0.8631	0.7905	0.82594	0.7077	0.6991
resnet50	0.8430	0.8145	0.8284	0.7059	0.7084
resnet101	0.8591	0.7040	0.7797	0.6557	0.6205
mobilenetv2	0.8520	0.6968	0.7726	0.6466	0.6106

In Fig. 15, two training and test labelled images together with the prediction result is illustrated using the resnet50 transferred network. Some of the prominent misclassified nan-farm pixels as farms (FN) are the rivers and residential areas. The misclassified river can be seen in the test image. The rivers are very similar to the sharp edges connecting several farms and the tiny connected components as residential areas were segmented as farm areas. In addition, in the local patches, there are also parts of green areas that show some sharp corners similar to farms but different in color compared to the majority adjacent farms. They might be farms left uncultivated for some time and caused uncertainties in labeling stage and can also influence the accuracy of the models. That can be considered as one of the limitations low resolution images for appropriate labeling.

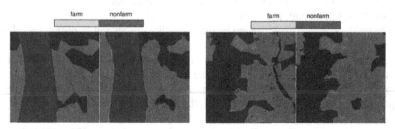

Fig. 15. From left to right, a ground truth labeled image for a training sample and the predicted labels, then a ground truth labeled image for a test sample and the predicted labels.

5 Conclusions

This paper is focused on farm detection using low resolution satellite images. The overall frame work consists of local patch or Region of Interest (ROI) classification followed by semantic segmentation of detected farm patches in order to find farm pixels. Two main patch classification strategies were employed in the first stage of the frame work; first a traditional hand-crafted feature extraction and modelling strategy was developed. In this method, unsupervised thresholding using Normalized Difference Moisture Index (NDMI) was used for green area detection. Then, a two-step algorithm was developed using Grey Level Co-occurrence Matrix (GLCM), 2D Discrete Cosine Transform (DCT) and morphological features as well as Support Vector Machine (SVM) modelling to discriminate the farms patches from other patches (non-textured or textured) that do not include any farm. The second patch classification strategy is based on deep high-level features learnt from the pre-trained Visual Geometry Group Network (VGG-16) networks. In order to use these features for farm classification, transfer learning strategies were employed. Then in the second stage of the framework, farm pixels were semantically segmented from the local patches. For this aim, the Tendales_farm data set was created by manual labelling of the images. The deepLabv3+ semantic segmentation modelling strategy based on transfer learning was employed. Four different pretrained networks, resnet18, resnet50, resnet101 and mobilenet together with labelled patches were used to retrain the networks. Experimental results showed that for the first stage of the framework, Convolutional Neural Networks (CNN) models are superior in terms of patch classification accuracy (99.55% and 96.76% for train and test respectively). For the second stage of the frame work, the resnet50 achieved the highest global accuracy for semantic segmentation (90.38% and 82.84% for train and test respectively).

References

1. Van Weyenberg, S., Thysen, I., Madsen, C., Vangeyte, J.: ICT-AGRI Country Report (2010)
2. Schmedtmann, J., Campagnolo, M.L.: Reliable crop identification with satellite imagery in the context of Common Agriculture Policy subsidy control. Remote Sens. **7**(7), 9325–9346 (2015)
3. Leslie, C.R., Serbina, L.O., Miller, H.M.: Landsat and Agriculture—Case Studies on the Uses and Benefits of Landsat Imagery in Agricultural Monitoring and Production: U.S. Geological Survey Open-File Report, p. 27 (2017)
4. Vorobiova, N.S.: Crops identification by using satellite images and algorithm for calculating estimates. In: CEUR Workshop Proceedings, pp. 419–427 (2016)
5. Canty, M.J., Nielsen, A.A.: Visualization and unsupervised classification of changes in multispectral satellite imagery. Int. J. Remote Sens. **27**, 3961–3975 (2006)
6. Tian, J., Cui, S., Reinartz, P.: Building change detection based on satellite stereo imagery and digital surface models. IEEE Trans. Geosci. Remote Sens. **52**, 406–417 (2014)
7. Rembold, F., Atzberger, C., Savin, I., Rojas, O.: Using low resolution satellite imagery for yield prediction and yield anomaly detection. Remote Sens. **5**, 1704–1733 (2013). https://doi.org/10.3390/rs5041704
8. Fisher, J.R.B., Acosta, E.A., Dennedy-Frank, P.J., Kroeger, T., Boucher, T.M.: Impact of satellite imagery spatial resolution on land use classification accuracy and modeled water quality. Remote Sens. Ecol. Conserv. **4**, 137–149 (2018)
9. Lee, L.W., Francisco, S.: Perceptual information processing system, U.S. Patent 10 618 543 (2004)
10. Hossain, M.D., Chen, D.: Segmentation for Object-Based Image Analysis (OBIA): a review of algorithms and challenges from remote sensing perspective. ISPRS J. Photogramm. Remote Sens. **150**, 115–134 (2019)
11. Blaschke, T.: Object based image analysis for remote sensing. ISPRS J. Photogramm. Remote Sens. **65**, 2–16 (2010)
12. Paola, J.D., Schowengerdt, R.A.: The effect of neural-network structure on a classification. Am. Soc. Photogramm. Remote Sens. **63**, 535–544 (1997)
13. Hansen, M., Dubayah, R., Defries, R.: Classification trees: an alternative to traditional land cover classifiers. Int. J. Remote Sens. **17**(5), 1075–1081 (1996)
14. Hardin, P.J.: Parametric and nearest-neighbor methods for hybrid classification: a comparison of pixel assignment accuracy. Photogramtnetric Eng. Remote Sens. **60**(12), 1439–1448 (1994)
15. Foody, G.M., Cox, D.P.: Sub-pixel land cover composition estimation using a linear mixture model and fuzzy membership functions. Int. J. Remote Sens. **15**(3), 619–631 (1994)
16. Ryherd, S., Woodcock, C.: Combining spectral and texture data in the segmentation of remotely sensed images. Photogramm. Eng. Remote Sens. **62**(2), 181–194 (1996)
17. Stuckens, J., Coppin, P.R., Bauer, M.E.: Integrating contextual information with per-pixel classification for improved land cover classification. Rem. Sens. Environ. **71**(3), 282–296 (2000)
18. Lang, S.: Object-based image analysis for remote sensing applications: modeling reality – dealing with complexity. In: Blaschke, T., Lang, S., Hay, G.J. (eds.) Object-Based Image Analysis. LNGC. Springer, Heidelberg (2008). https://doi.org/10.1007/978-3-540-77058-9_1
19. Mountrakis, G., Im, J., Ogole, C.: Support vector machines in remote sensing: a review. ISPRS J. Photogramm. Remote Sens. **66**, 247–259 (2011)
20. Su, T., Zhang, S.: Local and global evaluation for remote sensing image segmentation. ISPRS J. Photogramm. Remote Sens. **130**, 256–276 (2017)

21. Juniati, E., Arrofiqoh, E.N.: Comparison of pixel-based and object-based classification using parameters and non-parameters approach for the pattern consistency of multi scale landcover. In: ISPRS Archives, pp. 765–771. International Society for Photogrammetry and Remote Sensing (2017)
22. Lu, D., Weng, Q.: A survey of image classification methods and techniques for improving classification performance. Int. J. Remote Sens. **28**(5), 823–870 (2007)
23. Zhang, L., Yang, K.: Region-of-interest extraction based on frequency domain analysis and salient region detection for remote sensing image. IEEE Geosci. Remote Sens. Lett. **11**, 916–920 (2014)
24. Zhang, L., Li, A., Zhang, Z., Yang, K.: Global and local saliency analysis for the extraction of residential areas in high-spatial-resolution remote sensing image. IEEE Trans. Geosci. Remote Sens. **54**, 3750–3763 (2016)
25. Han, J., Zhang, D., Cheng, G., Guo, L., Ren, J.: Object detection in optical remote sensing images based on weakly supervised learning and high-level feature learning. IEEE Trans. Geosci. Remote Sens. **53**, 3325–3337 (2015)
26. Fu, G., Liu, C., Zhou, R., Sun, T., Zhang, Q.: Classification for high resolution remote sensing imagery using a fully convolutional network. Remote Sens. **9**, 1–21 (2017). https://doi.org/10.3390/rs9050498
27. Muhammad, U., Wang, W., Chattha, S.P., Ali, S.: Pre-trained VGGNet architecture for remote-sensing image scene classification. In: Proceedings - International Conference on Pattern Recognition, August 2018, pp. 1622–1627 (2018)
28. Albert, A., Kaur, J., Gonzalez, M.C.: Using convolutional networks and satellite imagery to identify patterns in urban environments at a large scale (2017)
29. Wu, M., Zhang, C., Liu, J., Zhou, L., Li, X.: Towards accurate high resolution satellite image semantic segmentation. IEEE Access **7**, 55609–55619 (2019). https://doi.org/10.1109/ACCESS.2019.2913442
30. Long, J., Shelhamer, E., Darrell, T.: Fully convolutional networks for semantic segmentation. In: IEEE Conference on Computer Vision and Pattern Recognition (CVPR), pp. 3431–3440 (2015)
31. Jégou, S., Drozdzal, M., Vazquez, D., Romero, A., Bengio, Y.: The one hundred layers tiramisu: fully convolutional densenets for semantic segmentation. In: IEEE Computer Vision and Pattern Recognition Workshops, pp. 11–19 (2017)
32. Chen, L.C., Yang, Y., Wang, J., Xu, W., Yuille, A.L.: Attention to scale: scale-aware semantic image segmentation. In: IEEE Conference on Computer Vision and Pattern Recognition (CVPR), pp. 3640–3649 (2016)
33. Wei, Y., Feng, J., Liang, X., Cheng, M.M., Zhao, Y., Yan, S.: Object region mining with adversarial erasing: a simple classification to semantic segmentation approach. In: IEEE Conference on Computer Vision and Pattern Recognition (CVPR), pp. 1568–1576 (2017)
34. Ronneberger, O., Fischer, P., Brox, T.: U-Net: convolutional networks for biomedical image segmentation. In: Navab, N., Hornegger, J., Wells, W.M., Frangi, A.F. (eds.) MICCAI 2015. LNCS, vol. 9351, pp. 234–241. Springer, Cham (2015). https://doi.org/10.1007/978-3-319-24574-4_28
35. Volpi, M., Tuia, D.: Dense semantic labeling of subdecimeter resolution images with convolutional neural networks. IEEE Trans. Geosci. Remote Sens. **55**, 881–893 (2017). https://doi.org/10.1109/TGRS.2016.2616585
36. Culurciello, A.C.: LinkNet: exploiting encoder representations for efficient semantic segmentation. In: IEEE Visual Communications and Image Processing (VCIP) (2017)
37. He, K., Sun, J.: Deep residual learning for image recognition. In: 2016 IEEE Conference on Computer Vision and Pattern Recognition (CVPR), pp. 770–778 (2016). https://doi.org/10.1109/CVPR.2016.90

38. Chen, L.-C., Papandreou, G., Schroff, F., Adam, H.: Rethinking atrous convolution for semantic image segmentation (2017). arXiv:1706.05587

39. Chen, L., Zhu, Y., Papandreou, G., Schroff, F.: Encoder-decoder with atrous separable convolution for semantic image segmentation

40. Sharifzadeh, S., Tata, J., Tan, B.: Farm detection based on deep convolutional neural nets and semi- supervised green texture detection using VIS-NIR satellite image important topic in digital agriculture domain. In: Data2019, pp. 100–108 (2019)

41. Bouvrie, J., Ezzat, T., Poggio, T.: Localized spectro-temporal cepstral analysis of speech. In: Proceedings of International Conference on Acoustics, Speech and Signal Processing, pp. 4733–4736 (2008)

42. Sharifzadeh, S., Skytte, J.L., Clemmensen, L.H., Ersboll, B.K.: DCT-based characterization of milk products using diffuse reflectance images. In: 2013 18th International Conference on Digital Signal Processing, DSP 2013 (2013)

43. Sharifzadeh, S., Serrano, J., Carrabina, J.: Spectro-temporal analysis of speech for Spanish phoneme recognition. In: 2012 19th International Conference on Systems, Signals and Image Processing, IWSSIP 2012 (2012)

44. Landsat.usgs.gov. Landsat 8 | Landsat Missions. https://landsat.usgs.gov. Accessed 17 May 2018

45. Ali, A.: Comparison of Strengths and Weaknesses of NDVI and Landscape-Ecological Mapping Techniques for Developing an Integrated Land Use Mapping Approach. A case study of the Mekong delta, Vietnam (2009)

46. Ji, L., Zhang, L., Wylie, B.K., Rover, J.: On the terminology of the spectral vegetation index $(NIR − SWIR)/(NIR + SWIR)$. Int. J. Remote Sens. **32**, 6901–6909 (2011)

47. Li, B., Ti, C., Zhao, Y., Yan, X.: Estimating soil moisture with Landsat data and its application in extracting the spatial distribution of winter flooded paddies. Remote Sens. **8**, 38 (2016)

48. Gao, B.: NDWI—a normalized difference water index for remote sensing of vegetation liquid water from space. Remote Sens. Environ. **266**, 257–266 (1996)

49. Tuceryan, M.: Moment based texture segmentation. In: Proceedings - International Conference on Pattern Recognition, pp. 45–48. Institute of Electrical and Electronics Engineers Inc. (1992)

50. MATLAB: Graycomatrix

51. Haralick, R.M., Dinstein, I., Shanmugam, K.: Textural features for image classification. IEEE Trans. Syst. Man Cybern. **6**, 610–621 (1973)

52. Chang, C., Lin, C.: LIBSVM: a library for support vector machines. ACM Trans. Intel. Syst. Technol. (TIST). **2**, 1–39 (2011)

53. Hastie, T., Tibshirani, R., Friedman, J.: The Elements of Statistical Learning. Springer, New York (2009). https://doi.org/10.1007/978-0-387-84858-7

54. Petropoulos, G.P., Kalaitzidis, C., Prasad Vadrevu, K.: Support vector machines and object-based classification for obtaining land-use/cover cartography from Hyperion hyperspectral imagery. Comput. Geosci. **41**, 99–107 (2012)

55. Li, E., Xia, J., Du, P., Lin, C., Samat, A.: Integrating multilayer features of convolutional neural networks for remote sensing scene classification. IEEE Trans. Geosci. Remote Sens. **55**(10), 5653–5665 (2017)

56. Chaib, S., Liu, H., Gu, Y., Yao, H.: Deep feature fusion for VHR remote sensing scene classification. IEEE Trans. Geosci. Remote Sens. **55**, 4775–4784 (2017)

57. Image Net. http://www.image-net.org/. Accessed 12 Jan 2019

58. Chen, L.-C., Papandreou, G., Kokkinos, I., Murphy, K., Yuille, A.L.: Deeplab: semantic image segmentation with deep convolutional nets, atrous convolution, and fully connected crfs (2016). arXiv:1606.00915

59. Zheng, S., et al.: Conditional random fields as recurrent neural networks. In: ICCV (2015)

60. Zhao, H., Shi, J., Qi, X., Wang, X., Jia, J.: Pyramid scene parsing network (2016). arXiv: 1612.01105
61. Fu, J., Liu, J., Wang, Y., Lu, H.: Stacked deconvolutional network for semantic segmentation (2017). arXiv:1708.04943
62. Zhang, Z., Zhang, X., Peng, C., Cheng, D., Sun, J.: Enhancing feature fusion for semantic segmentation (2018). arXiv:1804.03821

About the Fairness of Database Performance Comparisons

Uwe Hohenstein$^{(\boxtimes)}$ and Martin Jergler$^{(\boxtimes)}$

Corporate Technology, Siemens AG, Otto-Hahn-Ring 6, 81730 Munich, Germany
{Uwe.Hohenstein,Martin.Jergler}@siemens.com

Abstract. Whenever a new database technology appears, several comparisons also come up to attest that the new database technology is better than the traditional relational one. Even more, an outstanding performance is shown quite often by conducting performance comparisons. This paper attempts to illustrate that these performance comparisons should be taken with a pinch of salt. Revisiting published statements about comparisons between the Neo4j graph database and relational systems, we investigate several causes why relational systems show a worse performance. One possible reason is – among others – applying a default database configuration or configuring the system inadequately. Next, most tests are implemented in a straightforward manner, particularly not considering alternatives or applying useful features. In order to support our findings, we use a PostgreSQL database and implement some scenarios that are commonly used in comparisons. Thereby, we invalidate some stated results about the bad performance of relational systems in those scenarios. Concluding the discussion, we present some general considerations how fairness of comparisons can be improved.

Keywords: Performance · Comparison · Benchmark · Neo4j · PostgreSQL

1 Introduction

New database technologies are regularly entering the database market to compete with traditional relational database management systems (RDBMSs). In the 90s, object-oriented DBMSs implemented a new way to store objects in C++ or Java including their related objects on physical disk more or less directly. Moreover, they claimed a much higher performance than RDBMSs and aimed at substituting them. Many benchmarks, for example OO1 and OO7 [4] among others, showed the superiority. A little time later, XML databases concentrate on storing and retrieving XML documents efficiently. More recently, the NoSQL movement has attracted a lot of interest since 2009. The acronym NoSQL has been selected to indicate a deviation from SQL-based RDBMSs, although NoSQL should nowadays be understood as "not only SQL" (http://www.nosql-database.org). In general, NoSQL covers new approaches macerating relational concepts such as strong consistency that seemed to be settled for decades. NoSQL comes with several categories and many products within each category. One category of products attempts to better scale with large amounts of data by using a large amount of commodity computers and to benefit from distribution. Others use different internal structures to store complex graph structures in a specialized graph database etc.

© Springer Nature Switzerland AG 2020
S. Hammoudi et al. (Eds.): DATA 2019, CCIS 1255, pp. 136–156, 2020.
https://doi.org/10.1007/978-3-030-54595-6_8

The promoters of every new technology predicate that their systems are better than traditional RDBMSs. The literature contains many discussions about technologies and comparisons between NoSQL and SQL, some of which are quite emotional and are referred to techno-religious debates by Moran [12]. In fact, those discussions are shallower than really focusing on technical issues. However, some deeper technical performance comparisons exist with many enthusiastic statements (see also [6]), for instance for the subcategory of graph databases such as:

- "The main benefit of native graph databases are performance and scalability" [9]
- "Graph databases outperform RDBMS on connected data" [10]
- "While MySQL did not finish within 2 h, Neo4j finished a traversal in less than 15 min" [14]
- "So the graph database was 1000 times faster for this particular use case" [1].

Those statements emphasize that graph databases are superior to traditional RDBMSs. Accompanying performance measurements underline the advantages. Certainly, graph databases follow an interesting approach and provide special features for handling graph structures that are useful for specific applications. However, we think that those statements are quite general and should be looked at carefully.

In this paper, we want to underline our assumption. We have already started an investigation in a previous paper [6]. This investigation is here extended by further test scenarios. Please note we do *not* want to argue that RDBMSs are still better than any other upcoming technology such as graph databases. Our intention is to investigate the unfairness of those statements and related performance comparisons. In particular, we aim at proving our point of view by measurements. We illustrate that many assumptions are disputable. For instance, many performance comparisons rely on default settings and ad-hoc configurations. While other technologies behave well, RDBMS heavily necessitate appropriate settings, e.g., for the database cache. Similarly, simple tuning such as creating indexes improve performance drastically, however, are usually not set in comparisons. Furthermore, other data structures than the obvious or traditional ones are advantageous and might affect performance just as implementing some logic in stored procedures instead of using SQL does. Moreover, the test scenarios and conditions such as testing only warm start-ups are questionable particularly if data sets do not completely fit into main memory.

We investigate in detail the huge impact of appropriately adjusting database configurations and simple tuning activities such as defining indexes compared to relying on ad-hoc configurations and settings. We also illustrate how performance can benefit from different table structures. Similarly, using stored procedures to program logic instead of sticking to pure SQL can improve performance dramatically. And finally, it must be understood what the tested scenario means. Indeed, similar scenarios, especially variants of a traversal, behave quite differently in terms of performance.

In the following, Sect. 2 gives a brief introduction into graph databases, particularly the Neo4j system, because we focus on typical Neo4j scenarios used for performance comparisons. Section 3 underpins the novelty of our investigation by discussing related work as far as it is relevant for our paper. In Sect. 4, we present our main concerns with fairness of performance comparisons and summarize some general influencing factors. Afterwards, we elaborate in Sect. 5 upon some commonly used Neo4j test scenarios for which we have performed performance measurements using a PostgreSQL database. In addition to our previous evaluation in [6], we discuss in Sect. 6 some further scenarios where table structures play an important role. Some criteria for achieving a fair performance comparison are conducted in Sect. 7. before the analysis is concluded in Sect. 8 by outlining some future work.

2 Principles of Neo4j

Graph databases are one of the NoSQL database types. They are often considered to perfectly fit to process large connected data sets because native graph databases maintain a natural adjacency index.

Neo4j [13] is a graph database that is based on the so-called property graph model. Neo4j stores data in a graph, the most generic form of data structure, being capable of elegantly representing any kind of data.

The Neo4j data model consists of nodes and relationships. Nodes possess properties and are mainly used to represent entities.

Relationships between nodes are the key feature of graph databases, as they allow for finding related data. A relationship connects two nodes and is guaranteed to have a valid source and target node. Relationships organize nodes into arbitrary richly inter-connected structures. A relationship might possess a direction and properties.

Relationships are traversable in either direction. A traversal is a typical way to query a graph, navigating from starting nodes to related nodes by following relationships. In spite of having a direction, there is no need to duplicate relationships in the opposite direction (with regard to traversal or performance).

Both nodes and relationships may have properties. Properties are named values where the name (or key) is a string. The supported property values can be numeric, strings, booleans, or lists of any of the above types.

A label in Neo4j assigns types to nodes. A label is a named graph construct that is used to group nodes into sets; all nodes labelled with the same label belong to the same logical set. Database queries can work with these sets instead of the whole graph, making queries easier to write and more efficient to execute. A node may be labelled with any number of labels, even none. Labels are also used for defining constraints and adding indexes for properties.

The query language Cypher provides a declarative way to query the graph powered by traversals and other techniques.

3 Related Work

In the literature, several performance investigations can be found. Indeed, we extracted enthusiastic statements and test scenarios from these sources in order to qualify them by using own implementations.

For example, Khan [10] explains that the technology of graph databases is better than RDBMSs because RDBMSs require joins that are bad for graph structures. The database schema he used consists of Employees (E), Payments (P), and Departments (D), which are related by one-to-many relationships E-P and D-E, resp. The scenario selects two departments first and determines the related employees (via D-E) and afterwards the payments (via E-P). The complexity is evaluated in Big-O notation. Depending on the join strategy used by the optimizer, RDBMSs achieve a complexity of $O(|E|+|P|)$ with hash joins and $O(|E|*|P|)$ with nested loop joins while Neo4j achieves a constant $O(k)$ behavior. The internals of Neo4j leading to a constant behavior are described by *"Using hash indexing this gives $O(1)$. Then the graph is walked to find all the relevant payments, by first visiting all employees in the departments, and through them, all relevant payments. If we assume that the number of payment results are k, then this approach takes $O(k)$."* Unfortunately, it is not explained how "visiting all employees" is implemented in Neo4j, what is special to the internal Neo4j data structures leading to the constant behavior compared to hash indexes in RDBMSs.

Adell [1] uses a friendship relationship connecting people to their friends. The friendship database is filled with 1,000,000 users with an average of 50 friends. The implemented scenario takes two arbitrary people and detects whether both are direct or indirect friends considering 4 or fewer hops. While the RDBMS was running several days and was finally stopped, Neo4j required only 2 ms for the check.

In a similar setup, Rodriguez [14] uses a database with 1,000,000 nodes and 4,000,000 arbitrarily selected edges with an average fan-out of 4. Traversing from a selected starting node, all related nodes that can be reached by 1 to 5 hops are determined. The performance comparison shows that Neo4j is more than twice as fast for 4 hops. While Neo4j found the nodes for 5 hops in 14.37 min, MySQL was stopped after 2 h.

Baach [2] uses two data sets with 100,000 and 1,000,000 nodes, resp. In either setup, each node possesses exactly 50 edges. Compared to the previous tests, Baach's implementation does not query all the nodes, but only *counts* the number of friends up to 5 hops. Surprisingly, Neo4j was about 6 times slower than MySQL. Baach presumes that the Cypher query language (CQL) used by him performs much worse than the Pipes framework used by Rodriguez [14]. Baach's opinion is that a comparison of query languages, SQL and CQL, is fair. Forcing RDBMS to use SQL while allowing Neo4j to benefit from an optimized Pipes framework seems to be unfair. Moreover, Baach spent some time configuring MySQL appropriately, which might be another explanation for the results.

Vicknair et al. [15] build a direct acyclic graph with data sets of 1,000, 5,000, 10,000 and 100,000 nodes. They perform several tests that traverse the graph and count the nodes, for 4 and 128 hops and determine all the orphan nodes. Moreover, they consider the payload, e.g., counting the number of nodes that exceed a certain payload value. Since the data sets are small, tests mainly measure in-memory processing. This particularly results in execution times less than 200 ms, without revealing notable differences between Neo4j and MySQL.

Real application scenarios are taken by the following work. Joishi and Sureka [8] and Martinez et al., [11] both compare the performance of MySQL and Neo4j. [8]

take two process-mining algorithms, e.g., analyzing causal dependencies between actors in carrying out a business process and finding similarities between actors based on the intersection of activities. It turned out that Neo4j attains a performance boost of a magnitude of $7\times$ over MySQL for the first scenario. However, Neo4j is 32 times slower than MySQL is for the similarity scenario.

Martinez et al. [11] perform 12 multi-join queries of a health application for three randomly generated data sets with 1,000, 10,000 and 100,000 entries. MySQL is faster than Neo4j for most of the queries but has a poor performance for larger data sets. It is important to note that indexes were not added in both database systems.

[9] compares Oracle 11g and Neo4j using a Medical Diagnostic System. The data set comprises about 28,000 patients, 625,721 patient visits, 869,666 patient-IssueMed records, to mention the main tables. Five count queries join two or three tables. While Oracle performs queries in a few seconds (depending on the query), Neo4j requires about 0.3 s.

All this work focuses on technical comparisons between technologies and products. However, this paper mistrusts the fairness of those comparisons. Indeed, only little work on unfairness of performance comparisons has been published so far. Baach [2] considers a comparison between a query language (SQL) and an optimized Neo4j framework instead of the Cypher query language as "*Comparing Neo4j to MySQL without the use of Cypher is comparing apples and oranges*". The Hacker forum [5] contains some critical statements remarking that many comparisons are bootless. To our knowledge, there is only one paper [7] that criticizes statements such as "ODBMSs are faster by factor 100" made in an evaluation of object-oriented database management systems (ODBMSs) for the OO7 benchmark [4]. In order to critically reflect the OO7 results, [7] conducted a case study. They transformed a real Oracle/C application into an ODBMS/C++ application and measured the performance of realistic scenarios for different ODBMSs. The results were stupendous and diverged from OO7 results since showing that only a single ODBMS-based implementation has the potential to be faster than the original Oracle-based solution, while one ODBMS was definitively much slower. Concluding that the best benchmark is the application itself, the paper suggests a methodology for deriving application-specific benchmarks.

4   Unfairness of Performance Comparisons

In the following, we explain why we think that published performance comparisons are unfair and should be seen with caution.

4.1   Scope of Comparison

As already outlined above, the existing literature on Neo4j contains many exciting claims about its performance. Khan et al. [9], for instance, shows that graph databases are superior to RDBMSs by applying a theoretical comparison of internal algorithms based on Big Os. However, he does not explain why the internal structures of Neo4j are better. A comparison of *technologies* at that level is neither valid nor expedient.

Similarly, a general comparison between a specific product X and class of systems as presented in [1] is wrong per se: Showing that Neo4j is faster than MySQL does not prove that Neo4j is faster than any relational system. There are many other relational products, too.

4.2 Small Test Data Sets

Oftentimes, performance tests are executed with rather small data sets, for instance, 1000, 5000, 10,000 records [15], and also graphs with 100,000 nodes [2] are not really large. The result of such experiment setups is basically a test of the in-memory capabilities of a system: All the data fits into the accordingly sized memory.

While such evaluation scenarios might be representative for certain applications, where all data fits into main memory, the results, however, cannot be generalized and applied to application scenarios with larger data sets, where cache misses are the norm and disk access is heavily involved.

4.3 Warm Start

In many systems, the first few query executions are slow because data must be fetched from disk to populate the cache and the query execution plan must be derived. Further executions, also with different values, are faster because the execution plan is already available and data is in the cache. For this reason, performance comparisons like [2] often first initialize the cache by fetching all the needed data in a warm start. Moreover, the cache size is perfectly adjusted. This sounds reasonable at a first glance, but usually not a few (tested) tables are used and accessed in real applications. Accesses to other tables will interfere and disturb the first cached data but remain untested. Hence, a warm start is representative only if all the data – not only that used in tests – fits into memory completely.

4.4 Using Standard Configurations

Database management systems have many configuration parameters such as the database cache size. Those parameters have a strong impact on performance. Looking into performance comparisons, however, mostly standard configurations are applied. For instance, Martinez et al. [11] notes that "The deployed database servers were not optimized" and "No index was added to the basic implementation".

Usually, the cache size, more precisely the size of the Java Virtual Machine, is configured for Neo4j to be large enough to keep most data in client-side memory. Instead, RDBMSs execute queries at server-side, which requires a different kind of cache configuration. Further parameters, for instance, the space for temporal data, affect sorting and eliminating duplicates. In fact, having configured all those parameters appropriately improves performance enormously.

4.5 Over-Tuning

Over-tuning means that a benchmark focuses on only a few scenarios of an application, which are then highly tuned for exactly that scenario. Those scenarios are over-tuned since other scenarios are not taken into account and might suffer from that particular tuning. A typical case is to focus on queries and maybe inserts while ignoring updates and deletes or mixed operation sets.

4.6 Artificial Test Scenarios

Most of the published benchmarks and comparisons are rather artificial: They use a configurable number of nodes and relationships (e.g., Vicknair et al. [15]), maybe a configurable fan-out for relationships. Using such a data set, they take traversals along connections between nodes as the typical use case. The main reason is conduct multiple tests with varying parameters in an easy manner thus keeping the effort for implementing and performing tests low. Barry [3] states that it is easy to spend $100,000 for benchmarking, especially if several systems should be compared with presumably different implementions. Those simplified tests help to reduce the implementation effort.

However, it is arguable whether those generic tests, which basically abstract from concrete applications, are able represent the behaviour of a concrete application by just configuring the parameters. Results of performance comparisons are only representative if tests coincide with the application in mind, i.e., if the amount of data and the distribution is similar as well as the access patterns. Or in other words, the tested operations must reflect the characteristic accesses of a given application. Configuring a couple of parameters generally do not let a benchmark represent the demands of a specific application. Indeed, benchmarks for graph databases are rather artificial in such a sense. Thus, it is usually impossible to adapt tests and their results by simply changing a few factors such as the number of nodes [2, 15] or the fan-out of relationships. Such a parameterization does not help to let a benchmark become more representative. It is a valid question whether simple and slightly configurable tests could be representative for an application at all.

Furthermore, performance comparisons focus on queries (i.e., traversals) and sometimes inserts. Corresponding tests are conducted independent of each other. Only little work considers updates and deletes or interleaving all those operations in one mixed scenario such as real-life applications do. Consequently, just a few features are compared in an isolated manner.

As already mentioned, traversals are the main scenario for graph databases. However, there are various interpretations what a traversal is. A traversal can be understood as selecting all connected nodes via up to n hops, or only counting the number of related nodes. Sometimes, all possible connections between two nodes are determined, while some other tests simply detect whether two nodes are related via up to n hops. These scenarios look quite similar, but we will illustrate later how huge differences in performance are. Anyway, such tests are scenarios that are advantageous for graph databases.

4.7   Implementation Issues

Most performance comparisons implement scenarios in pure SQL for RDMSs, ignoring the possibility to use stored procedures, for instance. Neo4j also provides a query language named Cypher QL, which is however often not used. Instead, tests are implemented in the procedural Neo4j Pipes framework which seems to yield better results as the test of Baach [2] reveals. Baach implemented a common scenario with the Neo4j Cypher query language, which was much slower than a comparable MySQL solution. Obviously, the Cypher language does not perform as well as the Pipes framework. Baach and we, too, think that comparing SQL with the Pipes framework is unfair. At least, RDBMSs should be given the freedom to choose an implementation language.

Similarly, most test implementations for a RDBMS apply a straightforward database schema. However, there are often other options using specific features, which should be tried out to improve performance.

4.8   Data Distribution

Beyond the chosen test scenarios and test data, especially the number of nodes and the number of edges, the distribution of data for individual nodes plays a crucial role for performance, too. For instance, the selected start node might have an impact on the result size because each node has a different number of related nodes over n hops. The best implementation solution can change when using different start and end nodes!

4.9   Evaluation

Even if a benchmark seems to be representative, the evaluation results may be unfair and may diminish the value of the results. Typically, several test scenarios for traversals, inserts, removals, queries are performed, being simple in nature and executed in isolation and independent of each other. Also, each test is often parameterized leading to several results.

Thus, a benchmark comprises a collection of independent results. This means particular performance values have to be somehow aggregated in order to get an overall result. Detailed analyses are possible, but it is questionable how to correctly extrapolate from results for simple operations to complex logic of the real application. A particular system is able to win a comparison by just aggregating and interpreting the results in the right way – a system might have won most test cases, have best average over all the test cases, be leading for some "relevant" weighting of test cases etc.

5   Performance Evaluation

The previously mentioned concerns frequently lead to published statements showing that graph databases are 100 times faster than traditional relational ones [1]. Indeed, these statements are quite general and must be seen relative to the test scenarios and the test implementations.

Thus, using common scenarios for Neo4j, we have implemented and performed some tests with a PostgreSQL database. We intentionally used an older version 9.5 because several comparisons of RDBMS vs. Neo4j are also older. This means that we did not take any advantage of using the most recent state of relational technology.

5.1 Scenarios

The published performance comparisons for Neo4j mainly use three "traversal" scenarios:

1. Scenario **ALL(n)** starts with a random node and determines all nodes reachable by less than n hops.
2. The **PATHS(n)** scenario computes only the paths between two given nodes related by k hops for $k \leq n$.
3. **EXISTS(n)** is not interested in the concrete paths, but checks whether two given nodes are related by k hops, $k \leq n$.

5.2 Test Conditions

All the tests we performed used the same laptop running Windows 7 with a dual-core processor, 12 GB of RAM, and a 465 GB SSD disk. We can certainly state that the machine is not oversized. Moreover, the tests ran in an isolated environment, i.e., no other application were running during our test, particularly no concurrent database accesses. Each test was performed 3 times. The average of measurements was taken.

It is important to note that we did not directly compare Neo4j with PostgreSQL since our main statement is that any comparisons are unfair anyway. Hence, we aim at putting some published statements into perspective.

We experimented with a database that contains 500,000 nodes with 50 edges to other randomly selected nodes. That is, using the commonly applied database schema of Adell [1] for handling friendship relationships with one single table `Friends(id int, friend int)`, we keep 50*500,000 = 2,500,500 records in that table. This is more data than performance comparisons typically use. Both fields `id` and `friend` comprise the primary key of the `Friends` table. Each person (or node) is identified by a unique `id`; the foreign key `friend` is a reference (or edge) to a friend's id, i.e., all those records that refer to the same `id` form the collection of friends for that person.

5.3 Impact of Indexes for the PATHS Scenario

The goal of this first test is to illustrate the huge impact of setting up simple indexes. The test starts with a PostgreSQL standard configuration, i.e., particularly a very small database cache of 128 MB. The already mentioned `Friends(id, friend)` table structure of Adell [1] has been used for representing a friendship relationship.

We have implemented the scenario PATHS(5); the corresponding SQL query is presented in Fig. 1.

```
select f1.id, f2.id, f3.id, f4.id, f5.id, f5.friend
from Friends f1
join Friends f2 on f2.id=f1.friend
join Friends f3 on f3.id=f2.friend
join Friends f4 on f4.id=f3.friend
join Friends f5 on f5.id=f4.friend
where f1.id = :s and f5.friend = :e
union
select f1.id, f2.id, f3.id, f4.id, f4.friend, null
from Friends f1
join Friends f2 on f2.id=f1.friend
join Friends f3 on f3.id=f2.friend
join Friends f4 on f4.id=f3.friend
where f1.id = :s and f4.friend = :e
union
select f1.id, f2.id, f3.id, f3.friend, null, null
from Friends f1
join Friends f2 on f2.id=f1.friend
join Friends f3 on f3.id=f2.friend
where f1.id = :s and f3.friend = :e
union
select f1.id, f2.id, f2.friend, null, null, null
from Friends f1
join Friends f2 on f2.id=f1.friend
where f1.id = :s and f2.friend = :e
union
select f1.id, f1.friend, null, null, null, null
from Friends f1 where f1.id = :s and f1.friend = :e;
```

Fig. 1. SQL statement for Scenario PATHS(5).

The query computes the complete paths between a start and end node :s and :e, resp. The result includes all the intermediate nodes. As already mentioned in Subsect. 5.2, the first execution was done with a cold start after a restart of the computer. The same query was then immediately executed additional three times in the sense of a warm start taking the average of numbers ("Ø"); "stdev" denotes the standard deviation. In addition, the same query has been run another time with different start and end points (i.e., the "Second" column). Results are summarized in Table 1 for cold and warm start.

Table 1. PATHS(5) results for investigating indexes.

Index	Cold start		Warm start			
	First [s]		First [s]		Second [s]	
	Ø	stdev	Ø	stdev	Ø	stdev
No	62.88	3.26	59.67	0.60	60.25	1.74
Yes	23.78	5.27	4.54	1.55	6.43	1.17

The test results underline the huge impact of indexes on performance. In fact, it is not surprising that indexes are essential for RDBMSs to achieve an acceptable performance. The difference is even higher for a warm start. A lack of basic indexes – maybe due to a too naive implementation or a standard configuration (cf. Subsect. 4.4) – can heavily falsify benchmark results.

Due to the obvious need for indexes, all the further tests will be done with indexes.

5.4   Cold/Warm Start

Table 1 also shows the difference between a warm and cold start for PATHS(5). Most performance comparisons only apply a warm start scenario. The intention of this test is to investigate how the system behaves in case of freshly loading data from disk. This is relevant if not all the data fits in memory, which might be the case for larger applications.

The difference between cold and warm start is small for not applying any indexes; then, table data must be loaded anyway. However, there is a large difference between cold and warm start when using indexes.

Consequently, a test should not only be restricted to warm start setups (cf. Subsect. 4.3).

5.5   Implementation Variants

Beyond simple indexes, query tuning can have a large impact. We take Scenario EXISTS(5) that determines the existence of connections between two nodes. In contrast to the PATHS scenario, where all existing paths are collected, EXISTS only returns a Boolean – connected or not. We checked three possible queries:

1. The simplest one executes the query for PATHS (cf. Fig. 1). If the result is not empty, then there is a connection.
2. We can also add a LIMIT 1 clause at the end of the previous query in order to limit the result to just a single first connection or none.
3. In another alternative, a LIMIT 1 is added to each sub-query. This let the execution stop early after the first hit:

```
(select f5.friend … limit 1)
union … union
(select f1.friend … limit 1)
```

Table 2 illustrates the enormous speed-up for the last variant 3). Hence, searching for alternative implementations or queries can be very effective. Indeed, this modification is quite simple, but obviously very effective. Taking one straightforward solution does not give best results (cf. Subsect. 4.7).

Please note that there are no connections for 1 to 4 hops in our test data. Consequently, all the sub-queries are executed.

Table 2. Results for implementation variants.

Variant	Cold [s]		Warm [s]	
	Ø	stdev	Ø	stdev
1)	23.78	5.27	4.54	1.55
2)	19.81	1.61	4.79	1.07
3)	2.39	0.13	0.057	0.02

5.6 Larger Cache Size

As already mentioned, the default cache in PostgreSQL is far too small: 128 MB are just able to keep 5% of our table data (864 MB) and index data (1607 MB). As a consequence, many reads have to access the disk.

In another test setup, we thus increase the cache size to 1024 MB, i.e., by factor 8. Anyway, this is still not enough memory to keep all the table and index data.

Table 3. Results for smaller vs. larger cache.

Cache size	Cold [s]		Warm [s]	
	Ø	stdev	Ø	stdev
128 MB	23.78	5.27	4.54	1.55
1024 MB	25.58	0.92	0.46	0.03

The results for a larger cache are presented in Table 3 for the PATHS(5) scenario. For a cold start, the difference between a default and large cache is very small because data must be fetched from disk anyway. However, for a warm start, we detect more than factor 8 of speed up. This means that sticking to default configurations does not yield correct performance numbers (cf. Subsect. 4.4).

Please note there are many further database parameters that can be tuned. For example, increasing the temporal space can speed up sorting and duplicate elimination.

5.7   Different Implementations and Structures

Nearly all published performance comparisons use some straightforward table structures and pure SQL for "implementing" the comparison tests. However, there are alternatives for data structures and/or implementing the computation logic, which are usually not tried out (cf. Subsect. 4.7). A table Friends3 (id int, friend1 int, friend2 int, friend3 int) can be used to store up to three friends in one single row. If there are less than three friends, some columns are left empty. In case of more than three friends, one or more continuation records are stored with the same id.

More flexibility is obtained by using the native PostgreSQL array type. We use a table FriendsWithArray(id int, friends int[]) with an array-valued column instead of the "standard" table Friends (id, friend). Now, a single record represents one node. The array can keep an arbitrary and varying number of friends.

Using this table structure, we perform Scenario ALL. The following query retrieves the nodes reachable by less than four hops starting with a person :p:

```
select distinct f1.id as fid, f1.friends              -- (1)
into tmp3
from FriendsWithArray f1
where f1.id = :p;
insert into tmp3
select distinct f2.id, f2.friends
from FriendsWithArray f1, FriendsWithArray f2,
     generate_subscripts(f1.friends,1) i1,
where f1.id = :p and f1.friends[i1] = f2.id
union ... union
select distinct f4.id, f4.friends
from FriendsWithArray f1, FriendsWithArray f2,
        generate_subscripts(f1.friends,1) i1,
        generate_subscripts(f2.friends,1) i2,
        FriendsWithArray f3, FriendsWithArray f4,
        generate_subscripts(f3.friends,1) i3,
where f1.id = :p and f1.friends[i1] = f2.id
and f2.friends[i2] = f3.id and f3.friends[i3] = f4.id;
select distinct t3.id, friends[i] as friend           -- (2)
into tmp4
from tmp3 t3, generate_subscripts(t3.friends,1) i
```

Fig. 2. Query for the ALL(4) scenario with arrays.

f1.friends is an array that contains the friends of the 1st hop. The built-in function generate_subscripts is applied to an array-valued column and returns a set of indices to which a variable i can then be bound. The term friends[i] uses the variable i to access the i-th field in the array and is then used to join array elements (i.e., friends) and persons' ids, e.g., f1.friends[i1]=f2.id. The query of Fig. 2

stores the result in a temporary table `tmp3` (cf. (1) in Fig. 2). A stored procedure takes the temporary table and performs the next step (2) to unnest the node ids. The result is again stored in a temporary table `tmp4` to compute ALL(4).

This query can be extended to implement the ALL(5) scenario, i.e., all nodes with less than 5 hops, by two additional steps as shown in Fig. 3:

```
select f5.id, f5.friends
into tmp5
from FriendsWithArray f5, tmp4 t4
where f5.id = t4.friend;
select distinct t5.friends[i]   -- unnest
from tmp5 t5, generate_subscripts(t5.friends,1) i;
```

Fig. 3. Query for the ALL(5) scenario with arrays.

Table 4. Results for Scenario ALL.

Variant [s]	Small cache		Large cache	
	Ø	stdev	Ø	stdev
ALL(4) "Old"	16.43	3.21	16.28	2.87
ALL(4) "New"	8.76	3.54	4.54	1.98
ALL(5) "New"	28.67	3.26	24.55	1.75

Table 4 displays the improvement against the usual implementation. The test ALL(4) "New" refers to the new logic, while ALL(4) "Old" is computed with a single SQL query similar to Fig. 1, however, returning related nodes for a start node `:s` instead of paths (Fig. 4):

```
select f5.friend
from Friends f1
join Friends f2 on f2.id=f1.friend
join Friends f3 on f3.id=f2.friend
join Friends f4 on f4.id=f3.friend
join Friends f5 on f5.id=f4.friend
where f1.id = :s
union
select f4.friend from Friends f4 ... where f1.id = :s
union
select f3.friend from Friends f3 ... where f1.id = :s
union
select f2.friend from Friends f2 ... where f1.id = :s
union
select f1.friend from Friends f1 where f1.id = :s;
```

Fig. 4. Traditional 1-SQL-Query for the ALL(4) scenario.

There is a large difference for ALL(4) of factor 2 for the small and factor 4 for the large cache. What is even more important is that the computation of related nodes over 5 hops, i.e., ALL(5), is possible in the new implementation with about half a minute – as opposed to several hours as stated in [1, 14]. Hence, the new approach is performing well, however, the improved performance gain is paid by some drawbacks. The table violates the first normal form. Anyway, even the SQL standard introduced non-first-normal-form features. Moreover, the table structure is still easy (maybe even easier) to understand. What is more critical is that inserts and deletes become more complicated. Inserting a new relationship must add the friend to the array. Deleting a friend relationship must remove the friend from the array. A stored procedure might help to handle the logic.

5.8 Data Distribution

Another point is about choosing the (right) test data. There is again some impact on performance (cf. Subsect. 4.8). For instance, if we use PATHS(5) with different start and end nodes, we obtain different numbers of connections, and as a consequence, a different size of the result set. Table 5 illustrates the impact of using different start and end nodes. The smaller the number of retrieved connections is, the faster the query performs.

Table 5. Results for different result sizes.

Result size	Cold [s]		Warm [s]	
	Ø	stdev	Ø	stdev
479 recs	15.18	1.27	3.32	0.64
797 recs	23.78	5.27	4.54	1.55

The order of sub-queries is also relevant for the implementations of Scenario EXISTS(5) in Subsect. 5.5. If we know that there are no hop-1 and hop-2 but hop-3 connections between nodes in the test data, we should put the hop-3 sub-query in front in order to avoid the execution of sub-queries immediately. That is, knowing the data set, the implementation can be "improved". This is also a form of over-tuning (cf. Subsect. 4.5) by consciously "tuning" the order of sub-queries according to data.

In order to elaborate more on another facet of Subsect. 4.8, we use a larger database with 5,000,000 nodes each having four randomly chosen friends. Using the bad performing One-SQL-statement of ALL(n) based upon Fig. 1 with a large cache yields the results for $n = 9$ and $n = 10$ as shown in Table 6. Test ALL(9) returns 334,247 rows in 8 s, whereas ALL(10) yields 1,172,908 rows in 26 s with a warm start. With a cold start, execution times are a little slower. Anyway, even $n = 9$ and $n = 10$ achieve moderate execution times with the non-optimized One-SQL-statement query and the standard table structures despite the higher number of hops.

That is, compared to the previous database, the fan out seems to be one decisive factor for performance results, too (cf. Subsect. 4.8).

Table 6. Results for ALL scenario (5,000,000 nodes, large cache).

	Cold [s]		Warm [s]		Number of returned values
	Ø	stdev	Ø	stdev	
ALL(9)	20.66	0.22	8.01	0.05	334,247
ALL(10)	37.44	3.86	26.40	0.41	1,172,908

5.9   Differences in Traversal Scenarios

In the previous tests, we have considered different scenarios that implement traversals. However, traversals have different interpretations, which we named ALL, PATHS, and EXISTS: returning all related nodes, all the paths between two given nodes, or determining whether a relationship exists between two persons. In particular, we recognize quite a different performance behavior of the interpretations of traversal scenarios. In a warm start, PATHS(5) is performed in about 5 s, while EXISTS(5) is even much faster (a few milliseconds) using an optimized query. However, finding nodes in ALL(5) is slow with half a minute in an optimized version while the straightforward solution takes some hours.

This discussion underlines the importance of the chosen scenario and its semantics, even if scenarios seemingly look very similar (cf. Subsect. 4.6).

5.10   JDBC Configuration

So far, we have performed tests with the PostgreSQL pgadmin console for interactive query processing, i.e., executing SQL or stored procedures interactively with a query browser. However, database access will usually be done in a programming language using JDBC, ADO.NET, an object/relational mapping tool such as Hibernate etc. Hence, another factor enters the game having impact on performance comparisons.

We consider fetching the query result in Java with JDBC. Again, there are several options. One important parameter in JDBC is the fetch size, which can be set by `set-FetchSize(n)`. The fetch size determines how many records are transferred from the database server to the client program: If a record is requested by the client, a bulk of n records is physically prefetched and transferred, already serving this and the next n − 1 successive requests, too. Any further request will then fetch the next bulk of n records.

We have used ALL(4) and executed the "Old", non-optimal query with different fetch sizes. The results are summarized in Table 7. The query executed in 30 s with a

Table 7. Results for ALL(4) scenario with different JDBC fetch sizes.

JDBC fetch size	Warm start	
	Ø	stdev
1	30.468	1.04
1000	18.309	1.21

size of 1 (typically being the default) and 18 s with a size of 1000. This a huge difference, especially since the query execution itself consumes about 15 s.

This a huge difference, especially since the query execution itself consumes about 15 s. Again, relying on some defaults affects the performance negatively (cf. Subsect. 4.4).

In case of Hibernate, a query is typically executed with

```
List result = session.createQuery("<query>").list();
```

Similar to JDBC, a fetch size can be configured with the same effect and behavior. It is important to note that the whole result is materialized in the `result` Java list. This obviously requires a lot of memory, especially for ALL(4) result sets with about 500,000 records, and even more for ALL(5).

An alternative is to apply some streaming of results where data is returned in a cursor-like fashion.

6   Further Considerations About Data Structures

There are often alternatives or optimizations as Subsect. 5.7 has already illustrated by using proprietary array-based columns. As another example, we want to reveal the typical relational structure for storing trees:

```
Tree(id, properties, fatherId)
```

The above table structure is commonly used but is often considered as inappropriate for querying whole subtrees. Starting with the sons of a given father node, the sons of each son have to be found recursively until the leaves are reached:

```
with recursive Sons (id, fatherId, lev) as
(select id,fatherId,1 from Tree where fatherId = :x
union
select t.id, t.fatherId, s.lev+1 from Tree t, Sons s
where t.fatherId=s.id
) select * from sons;
```

Such a query is said to perform badly due to the need of recursion. Another structure has been suggested in the literature:

```
Tree(id, properties, fatherId, firstLeft, lastRight)
```

`firstLeft` and `lastRight` are auxiliary columns that help to determine subtrees. Figure 5 illustrates the principle of setting these columns.

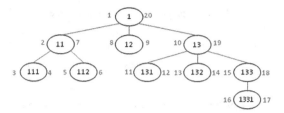

Fig. 5. Improved tree data structure for retrieval.

The idea is that `firstLeft` (left hand side of a node) and `lastRight` (right hand side) of a node determine the range of its subtree. To set the values, the tree is traversed in a depth-first manner, thereby passing each node twice, left and right. For example, node 13 possesses `firstLeft=10 and lastRight=19`. This means that the subtree of node 13 has values `firstLeft>=10 and lastRight<=19`. The subtree of node 11 lies between 2 and 7 analogously. Hence, in order to return the subtree of a node :x, the following query can be issued without any recursion:

```
select sub.*
from Tree t, Tree sub
where t.Id=:x -- to retrieve starting node
and sub.firstLeft >= t.firstLeft
and sub.lastRight <= t.lastRight
```

The condition for checking whether a node is a leaf node is simply:

```
sub.lastRight - sub.firstLeft = 1.
```

The total number of nodes can be computed by: `root.lastRight /2`.

This structure is supposed to optimize the performance of common tree operations at the expense of maintaining the ordering for inserts, deletes, and movements by updating `firstLeft` and `lastRight` columns of many nodes.

Another possibility is to attach a path to each node. Starting with 1/ for the root, the sons of the root obtain a path 1/1, 1/2 etc. The next level contains three path elements accordingly. Concerning retrieval, the subtree for node i/j/k can be queried by LIKE 'i/j/k/%'. The effort to maintain the schema is moderate since deletions and updates do not require any action. Moving a node in the hierarchy requires computing and changing the path of that node only. For inserts, the largest value for siblings has to be determined and incremented to a path.

We made some performance measurements for retrieving subtrees at various levels. The results are summarized in Table 8 for a tree fanout of 5 and a depth of 10 with a total number of 12,207,031 nodes. The recursive query turned out to be the fasted for choosing a start node at any level, maybe because of the small fanout, the number of levels, or the equal distribution (see Subsect. 4.8). One particular reason why the path expression solution behaves worse is that the index on the path expression is not used; unfortunately, PostgreSQL cannot be forced to use the index.

Table 8. Variants for determining subtrees.

Level	Returned nodes	Variant [ms]		
		Recursive	Left/right	Path
3	488280	12,695	29,037	35,140
4	97655	2,581	6,466	11,821
5	19530	556	1,867	7,413
6	3905	103	850	6,679
7	780	40	694	6,371
8	155	13	592	6,233

7 Some Thoughts About Improving Fairness

So far, we have discussed some typical performance scenarios that have been published for graph databases by revealing tests with a PostgreSQL database. As shown, it is easily possible to achieve different – better – results than presented in the literature.

Now, we turn to the question how to improve fairness of performance comparisons.

First of all, it is an absolute precondition for fairness to supply the same environment, especially the same amount of resources such as hardware, processor, network, operating system, disks, RAM etc. Furthermore, there should be the same test isolation and the same overall test conditions etc.

However, it is becoming unfair if the size of memory for the database system is pinned. For instance, Neo4j is Java-based and execute queries at the client, making a lot of memory in the JVM more advantageous, while RDBMSs process queries in the server instead. Hence, a smaller JVM spares more RAM for the database system. Since the settings do not only depend on an application and its data, but also on the type of DBMS resources, resources cannot be set equally for all the test candidates.

The rules for conducting comparisons are also important. In principle, every test should implement the *same universe of discourse* with the same functionality. Conditions must not be too restrictive. But a tester should not be forced to use a specific database schema, a query language etc. For example, benchmarks for object-oriented database systems, e.g., [4] often dictated testers the same neutral implementation. Instead, there should be freedom for using SQL or not.

The execution of benchmarks or tests often relies on default configurations. Parameters such as the database cache size are set to default or configured at the most at good guess; tuning is more or less neglected. The OO7 benchmark [4] sanctifies this by noting that normal programmers are unable to tune a database system effectively. In our opinion, this proceeding is arguable if ease of use is not an issue. Most database systems *do* require an appropriate tuning in order to achieve an acceptable performance. Especially, RDBMSs heavily rely on indexes for primary and foreign key. Indeed, we have demonstrated how even simple tuning measures like creating indexes already improve performance substantially. Usually, there are much more screws to turn. This potential must be used for sustainable results.

Performance comparisons are fair if each tester obtains infinite time for implementing and also improving and tuning. However, since this seems to be infeasible in practice, the following attenuation makes sense: Each tester of a particular system should obtain equal and adequate time. The available time limit must not be too short. This enables programmers to try out several variants and to tune the overall system instead of choosing too straightforward, often naive solutions. If implementers do not possess the same degree of skills and knowledge, the skills should also be taken into account for restricting the time.

Finally, realistic and holistic test scenarios are indispensable. That is, scenarios should cover all the relevant use cases, particularly, representative and complete use cases with a mixed set of operations. Especially holistic scenarios help alleviate the risk of over-tuning or overemphasizing a particular operation, while ignoring other non-tested ones.

8 Conclusions

Whenever a new database technology arises, publications about more or less technical performance comparisons usually occur, too, proving that these technologies are superior to traditional relational database systems (RDBMSs) for various test scenarios.

In this paper, we focused on some exciting statements made for the graph database Neo4j. There are many published comparisons showing that Neo4j has huge performance gains compared to relational systems. We think that those statements are mostly unfair due to several reasons, which we discussed in the paper in depth. Moreover, those published performance comparisons motivated us to revisit some test scenarios common to those comparisons and to re-implement them using a PostgreSQL database. As one major result, this paper illustrated that performance varies drastically depending on several factors such as configuration, choice of database schemas, amount of data, simple tuning activities etc. for those scenarios for which RDBMSs were "proven" to be unsuitable and thus leading to a bad performance in published performance comparison. Instead, we were able to achieve good results for those critical scenarios quite easily by applying simple measures. As a consequence, selecting a database system should not be based upon blindly trusting published comparisons.

However, it was neither our intention to perform yet another performance comparison (which becomes unfair), nor to prove that relational systems are still better than graph databases. The message should not be that Neo4j is not faster than MySQL, Oracle,PostgreSQL or any other product, but rather than each system can be tuned for particular use cases in order to achieve an acceptable performance.

The main intention of this paper was thus to underline the necessity of independent benchmarks and comparisons with realistic and application-specific scenarios. A deeper investigation is indispensable for obtaining reliable and representative results. To this end, we tried to collect some recommendations to achieve fair performance comparisons.

In our future work, we intend to expand our investigation from graph databases to other NoSQL categories. In particular, we aim at analyzing other advantages of NoSQL products such as enhanced scalability by distribution, better flexibility by means of schema-less data structures etc.

References

1. Adell, J.: Performance of graph vs. relational databases (2013). https://dzone.com/articles/performance-graph-vs. Accessed 26 Nov 2019
2. Baach, J.: Neo4j performance compared to MySQL (2015). https://baach.de/Members/jhb/neo4j-performance-compared-to-mysql. Accessed 26 Nov 2019
3. Barry, D.: Should you take the plunge? Object Mag. **3**(6), 1994 (1994)
4. Carey, M., DeWitt, D., Naughton, J.: The OO7 benchmark. ACM SIGMOD **22**, 12–21 (1994)
5. Hacker. NoSQL vs. RDBMS: let the flames begin (2010). https://news.ycombinator.com/item?id=1221598. Accessed 26 Nov 2019
6. Hohenstein, U., Jergler, M.: Database performance comparisons: an inspection of fairness. In: 8th International Conference on Data Science, Technology and Applications DATA 2019, Prague, Czech Republic, June 2019
7. Hohenstein, U., Pleßer, V., Heller, R.: Evaluating the performance of object-oriented database systems by means of a concrete application. In: 8th DEXA Workshop, Toulouse (1997)
8. Joishi, J., Sureka, A.: Graph or relational databases: a speed comparison for process mining algorithm. In: Proceedings of 19th International Database Engineering & Applications Symposium, Yokohama (2015)
9. Khan, W., Ahmed, W., Shahzad, E.: Predictive performance comparison analysis of relational & NoSQL graph databases. Int. J. Adv. Comput. Sci. Appl. **8**(5), 523–530 (2017)
10. Khan, Q.: Why graph databases outperform RDBMS on connected data (2016). https://dzone.com/articles/why-are-native-graph-databases-more-efficient-than. Accessed 26 Nov 2019
11. Martinez, A., Mora, R., Alvarado, D., et al.: A comparison between a relational database and a graph database in the context of a personalized cancer treatment application. In: Proceedings of Alberto Mendelzon International Workshop on Foundations of Data Management, Panama City (2016)
12. Moran, B.: RDBMS vs. NoSQL: and the winner is …. (2010). http://www.itprotoday.com/microsoft-sql-server/rdbms-vs-nosql-and-winner. Accessed 26 Nov 2019
13. Neo4j. Neo4j (2019). www.neo4j.org
14. Rodriguez, M.: MySQL vs. Neo4j on a large-scale graph traversal (2011). https://dzone.com/articles/mysql-vs-neo4j-large-scale. Accessed 26 Nov 2019
15. Vicknair, C., Macias, M., Nan, X., et al.: A Comparison between a graph and a relational database: a data provenance view. In: Proceedings of 48th Annual Southeast Regional Conference, Oxford, USA (2010)

Author Index

Printed in the United States
By Bookmasters